Strategies for Profiting on Every Trade

Oliver L. Velez
with **Paul Lange**

Marketplace Books
Columbia, Maryland

Library of Congress Cataloging-in-Publication Data
Velez, Oliver L.
  Strategies for Profiting on Every Trade: Simple Lessons for Mastering the Market / written by Oliver L. Velez and Paul Lange.
     p. cm.
  Includes index.
  ISBN-13: 978-1-59280-259-3 (hardcover)
  ISBN-10: 1-59280-259-1 (hardcover)
  1. Portfolio management. 2. Investment analysis. 3. Stocks. 4. Electronic trading of securities. I. Lange, Paul, 1959- II. Title.
HG4529.5.V45 2006
332.64--dc22
                                                        2006039227

This book is dedicated to my lovely, ever patient
wife, Brenda, and my six amazing children,
Victoria, Jonathan, Rebecca, Oliver, Jr., and
the twins, Megan and Morgan.

Preface

One measure of writing for traders and investors (as perhaps with writing for all others), is the ah ha! factor—a sentence or thought that provokes a feeling of enlightenment or deep understanding with the reader. Our hope is for numerous ah ha! moments to occur in these pages.

Trading is a somewhat difficult subject to write about. As you learn and assimilate certain truths, these truths often can and should change for you later. What seemed quite profound to you at one time might seem a year later to be obvious—and no longer worthy of being mentioned. What has happened is that you have moved beyond this particular truth to a newer truth, a higher truth. In such fashion, the growing trader keeps moving beyond his own knowledge, outdating it.

At the same time, to someone new to the game of trading, these are still new truths, capable of changing one's thinking and approach, so in that sense, one is wrong not to include them. The bottom line is that a trader's approach continuously changes and evolves. Aside from the very newest beginners, and the most experienced traders, almost everyone in the market is at a different level of knowledge.

While I can't honestly say that *Strategies for Profiting on Every Trade* was written as a companion volume to my earlier book, *Tools and Tactics of the Master Day Trader* (McGraw Hill 2000), the reader of that earlier work will undoubtedly see a continuation of some of the ideas expressed in that book. *Tools and Tactics* dealt more with the psychology of the trader—his emotions, motivations, and frustrations—*Strategies for Profiting* focuses more on the game or activity itself.

This book is designed to address the needs of both income and wealth producing traders. There is a strong tendency to separate these two styles of trading into completely independent skill sets and approaches. But it is our view that not only can they not be split, but any attempt to do so would result in automatically curtailing your progress as a trader. In the same way that it is commonly understood that both your left and your right hand play equally crucial roles in everyday life, so do income trading and wealth trading play equally important roles in the daily lives of most successful traders. In other words, one should never chose whether the income producing style of trading is better than the wealth generating style, or visa-versa. Rather one should look to become adept at both styles. This book will teach you just how to accomplish that.

In chapter 1, Lessons on Getting Ready, you'll be guided in how a trader should prepare for each day and week. How you start will largely determine how you end in this business. I have witnessed far too many traders sloppily enter each week and each day without a plan and without a proper list of stocks to watch. This will not be you, after this chapter is assimilated.

In chapter 2, "Lessons on Some Basics," you will learn some very crucial things, such as how to deal with the all-important first hour of trading. Not many traders know that the pent up demand or accumulated supply built up overnight often make the first hour of trading the most volatile. The first 30-minutes of trading in particular are very tricky. You'll learn how to deal with this all important time period and turn it into opportunity. Did you know there are nine other times during each day of which every trader should be acutely aware? These nine reversal times, as we like to refer to them, offer some unique opportunities for watchful traders. You'll also be taught how to deal with the vagaries of news and how it can affect your stocks for the positive and negative.

Chapter 3 deals with two of the most crucial aspects of proper trading, trade management and money management. The correct management of your position always hinges on several things: a favorable risk/reward ratio, a proper entry, and an intelligently selected price target. Each aspect of a properly executed trade will be reviewed in detail in this chapter.

The psychological aspect of trading represents 85 percent of the game, in my opinion. As market participants, we don't really trade stocks, options, bonds, futures, currencies or any other financial instrument, for that matter. In reality, we trade people, the people who own those things I just listed. For any of the above items to move, people have to make buy and sell decisions, and the peoples' buy and sell decisions are incited by emotions, namely greed and fear. In chapter 4, we talk about how a trader is to cope with these two dominant emotions and how he can use them for profitability. We also delve into the challenge of always needing to be right and explain how the loss of trades can be turned to your best advantage.

Chapters 5, 6 and 7, get to the meat and potatoes of our trading method. We'll delve deeply into the many chart patterns that we rely on every single day in the market. You'll learn about several highly reliable trading events that happen over and over again, the same way each time. We'll show you how you can turn these events into consistent profits. In these sections, we'll equip you with many of the same trading techniques that we've taught to major Wall Street firms and some of the country's top traders.

Lao-tzu said, "a journey of a thousand miles must begin with a single step." It is our belief that the book you now hold in your hands can be the single step that launches your journey to profitability. So read each lesson carefully, take notes, and be sure to keep a journal of the ah-ha! moments that strike you. I have always taught that it takes only the mastery of two or three reliable strategies to do extraordinarily well in the market. In these pages, you will find far, far more than that. Use them well!

Oliver Velez

❖❖❖

It was quite a privilege when Oliver Velez approached me to help write *Strategies for Profiting on Every Trade* for his worldwide following. You see, Oliver Velez has been my mentor since I began trading. But as much as it was a privilege, I knew it would also be a challenge because I was about to undertake a monumental task.

Many of these lessons have been taught to students worldwide over a span of 4 years. These lessons contain powerful information that goes far beyond the basics you may find in many introductory trading books. Looking back, though it was an incredible amount of work putting this vast amount of information together, I am very proud of the task that we completed.

Paul Lange

Strategies for Profiting on Every Trade

Introduction

Getting Started, Part 1

So, you want to know something more about trading. Or is it online stock buying? Or is it day trading? Or is it investing? Well, let's get a few terms straight.

First, we consider 'investing' something that is no longer a term that should be applied to the stock market. Invest in real estate, bonds, or gold, but not stocks. It implies a 'long term buy and hold with your eyes closed approach' that should no longer be used in the stock market. Most of today's large cap companies are in technology. These companies are subject to having their main product replaced by a new technology very easily. Long ago, it would have taken years for any company to start up a new car company and overtake General Motors. Today, anyone can create software in their garage that can revolutionize how something is done and consequently put a competitor out of business. Take the case of Iomega. The current technology at the time was storing information on 1.44 Meg disks. Iomega came out with a system to store 100 Megs on a disk, and got contracts to put their drive on every major computer. Sounds like a company you can buy and hold forever, doesn't it? It is, until someone discovers that the same information can go on a CD and have it cost much less. Then Iomega is gone, unless it has other products to sell. In today's marketplace companies must change or become extinct.

So if investing is out, what do we do? You hear stories about all of the 'day traders'. You look around you and you don't see many. You may not even know any besides yourself and those you met at a seminar. Unfortunately, the term 'day trading' is often misused by the media. There is a large group of people who we call 'online investors'. These are the folks who use their computers in place of their telephones to call places like E-Trade, Schwab, etc. and place their orders. They typically are managing their savings or IRA money, and are untrained. They were plentiful during the bull run of the 90's, and often were wrongly called 'day traders.' It did not matter because they made money during the bull market no matter what they did.

We consider ourselves day traders, or traders, but this does not include the much larger group of online traders mentioned above. We think of day traders as people who spend a good part of the day with the market; those who are trained to manage positions that may last from several minutes to several months. Though we believe that 'investing' is a dead term, we do use many time frames to hold stocks, the longest of which is a 'core' position. While a core position may last for months, it differs from investing because there is an exact exit strategy planned for a core position. We also use a 'swing' time frame. This is one that may last from two to five days. We also use tactics that would have us holding a stock overnight one time, or exiting the same day, or sometimes exiting part of a position only minutes after entry.

So if you are going to day trade, how do you buy stocks? If you are trading only a few trades a week, and limiting yourself to swing and core trades, it is fine to use one of the online brokers. The time it takes to have your order filled is not very fast, but for occasional long-term trades, it is acceptable. If you are going to be trading more often, or trading in and out the same day, you will want to use a direct access broker. This is a broker who lets you see all of the market participants, where they are buying, and where they are selling. You then place your own order via your web browser and many of these orders will have instant executions. By instant I mean within a fraction of a second.

So, you know what you want to do and have selected a broker. Now you need a computer and an Internet connection. Again, for occasional swing and core trading, any machine that can access the Internet will do. If you are going to be active intraday, you will need to have something better. You will need a powerful, top of the line computer and a fast Internet connection. Dial up access is no longer a realistic option. You need to be looking for DSL, Broadband, FIOS, Cable, Satellite, or T1-3. Depending on where you trade, you will have to evaluate which of these options is available and most effective for your money. You will need a working knowledge of computers because your time with the computer will be extensive whether or not you wish it to be.

Now you are ready to trade, right? Well, no, not really. The biggest distinction I made earlier was that day traders are educated in trading strategies and disciplines. This will be the focus of the next lesson, how to start out trading when you have no education or experience in trading. I will discuss how to build that education as you go, without using up all of your capital.

Getting Started, Part 2

In the last lesson, I discussed some basic things you need to review if you are going to start some form of trading. I would like to expand on those things and discuss in which time frames you may be interested in trading. Also, I will discuss how to get an education for varying costs and constraints.

Previously, I discussed the concept of time frames. Time is an important topic and is the next item you need to consider before you begin trading. The concepts of trading can be used to help people who are looking to better manage their IRAs. They can also be used for people trying to build wealth by swing trading investment money, and for people trying to produce income by trading on an intraday basis.

If you are going to be active in the markets, I recommend that you maintain two separate accounts for trading. These two accounts will have different goals. One account should be a wealth building account for core and swing positions. Core positions are positions based on weekly charts and can last from weeks to months. They have stop losses and entry points like any other trade. Targets may be set as an objective or left to an exit based on raised stops as the stock moves up (or lowered stops as stocks move down in the case of a short). Swing positions are based on daily charts and can last from two to five days. This wealth building account is important for capturing the major moves in the market. These are moves that may elude the trader who goes home flat every night. Gaps and large extended moves will benefit the swing and core trader, but often will only aggravate the intraday trader.

The second account should be income producing and should consist of day trades (ranging from minutes to all day), and guerilla trades. Guerilla trades are a special Pristine tactic. They are designed to capture fast moves in the market in one to two days. These strategies help maintain income flow even at times when the market may be moving sideways and not generating income in the wealth building account.

Once you decide on your time frame, you are ready to begin—not trading, but learning! Trading is one of the most challenging endeavors in which you can participate. Unfortunately, most traders will spend more time getting educated in the television market before buying a television than they will spend getting educated in trading concepts before buying a stock. Most traders do not feel the need to get educated in trading. Most traders also fail.

No one would try to be a doctor or a lawyer without the proper schooling. Yet for some reason, new traders believe that this is an easy to conquer profession. In fact, some of the smartest and most successful people often have the most difficult time trading. Also, continuous success, in other endeavors before trading often translates to overconfidence and stubbornness while trading: this is a bad combination. You must be able to admit when you are wrong and move on quickly. Successful people often are perfectionists—a quality not suited for trading. Good traders don't insist on being right—they aim to make money. ✸

Do you know right now, which strategies you want to play in this market? In this month? In this week? Today? Do you know which strategies you want to play at different times of the day? Do you know how to handle all of the market maker (a firm ready to buy and sell a particular stock on a regular and continuous basis at a publicly quoted price) tricks? Do you know how to handle reversal times? You see, the market is designed to extract money quickly from the unknowing. It is a game where very many supply much money to the very few. On which side of this equation have you been?

You need to develop a trading plan that outlines your total business plan when it comes to how you want to trade. You need to outline the strategies you want to use, and when you want to use them. You need to outline money management rules. How much will you risk on that scalp? How much on that core trade? How much can you afford to lose in one day? You need to understand trading and all the concepts it involves. This is the single most important step to successful trading. Yet, the vast majority of new traders do not have a plan.

Everyone has a different level of money and time they can devote to learning. That is fine: there are different ways to approach education. Some want to improve their core trading to help the returns of their IRAs while they work full time at their jobs. Some have come into some money and want to make their living trading the markets full time. Most traders lose too much in the beginning that cannot be regained by the time they decide to get an education. Don't let this happen to you. ✸✸

There are many opportunities to learn trading on many different time horizons and cost levels. Remember, you will pay for your education one way or another. Some traders lose more money in a week than it would take to get a good start on an education. Don't be one of those people who think, "When I make enough money trading to pay for a seminar, I will take it then…." Think of the logic in that statement. The training must come first.

Getting Started, Part 3

Okay, you caught me. If you read the first two lessons, it was clear that the intent was to have part one and part two. However, if Sylvester Stallone can make 6 Rocky movies, I can write a third beginner's lesson. Though they had a great deal of information, the lessons really only guided new people up to the day they start trading—not really a good time to leave them hanging.

Once you have made all the decisions discussed in the first two lessons and received an education to the level you feel you need to begin trading, the moment of truth arrives. I would like to make sure you have a few tools in your belt when you begin trading. First of all, there is a steep learning curve in trading. I urge you to start by paper trading. Get used to your trading software. Understand the plays. Begin to pick your favorites and really develop your trading plan. At this point, it is likely just a shell. Know how to get in and out of trades. The odds are that you will lose in the beginning. You are learning to apply what you have learned. You will make mistakes. So, do you want to have all this learning cost you real money or paper money?

How long should you paper trade? Until you are good at it. Really good. I have never met someone who admitted losing money paper trading. Set up criteria that you must pass to advance. You can use the criteria of making a certain number of points a day or possibly a certain number of days in a row of winning points, or x trades in a row without a loser. The criteria are not as important as following what you pick. When you are ready, move up to a small amount of risk. Start with about $50.00. You will notice the difference. Just the official beginning of your trading record and the pressure of real executions will really play with your head. Don't worry about making money yet: you will not, because of commissions. Worry about making money before commissions. Increase the risk amount slowly, and only upon passing the criteria you have set for yourself.

A word of warning: it is at this time that traders feel the pain of some small losses. Their first instinct is to increase their share size to recover their losses. The irony is obvious when you read this, but maybe not if it happens to you. Don't increase your share size until you trade well at your current level. It is always harder to trade with more shares.

During this process, you should be developing a trading plan. One that outlines the types of plays you will look for. It should restrict you from trading certain times and plays that you do not want to trade. It should outline money management rules for you, for handling both winning and losing days. It should set up your share size rules, and it should dictate what kind of record keeping, analysis, and continuing education you pursue.

Pay attention to the analysis part and make plans to follow up on all of your trades. Most traders spend 90 percent of their time trading, 10 percent on preparation, and 0 percent on follow up. This is a very big mistake. Traders should spend as much time following up on trades as they do trading. That does not mean that the time from 9:00 to 4:30 must be counted as trading time. Your plan may call for you to trade only the first and last hour. The time in between could be used to review the morning trades and prepare for the next day, paper trade new ideas, etc. You should spend considerable time printing charts of the trades you make, evaluating them, and learning from any mistakes. Good traders understand that the money lost when making a bad trade can be an investment in a process that works to eliminate mistakes and improve trading.

Good traders also understand that the market is always right, and the best we can do is play the odds. Be flexible and remember that even the best trades can be stopped out.

Strategies for Profiting on Every Trade

Chapter One
Lessons on Getting Ready

Developing a Watch List

There are many different styles of trading, and different traders prepare for the market in different ways. Most traders who do more than micro scalping start off the day with some kind of watch list. This list and its preparation will vary greatly. Here are some ideas of different ways to prepare for the next day.

To prepare for the next day, you will want to look at daily charts after the market closes. If you are swing trading, you live off of the daily charts. If core trading, you live off of the daily and weekly charts. Even if you are intraday only, you will put the odds more in your favor if you have multiple time frames all going in your direction. In other words, even if you were trading intraday, would you want the stock you are playing long to be a short set up on the daily? Of course not. Start with a list of long stocks to play long, even if intraday. If you trade from a small universe of favorites, at least categorize each trend as up, down, or sideways.

TRADE WITH THE TREND.

The first list that is the easiest to develop is of favorite stocks that you play every day. This list may include as few as 4 or 5 stocks, or up to 30 or 40. The number does not matter: the point is that the list consists of a handful of stocks that the trader knows very well. Many traders are successful doing this. There is a big advantage because they are familiar with every stock on their list. It is likely that they all trade well, are heavy volume, and easy to get in and out of without much slippage (paying more than the strike price to get into a long position because of the bid-ask spread or small volume on the offer). There is also a big disadvantage. You will miss many strategies that day. Your small list will not often have a mortgage play, or a nice bullish gap surprise.

Stock Screener Another easy list alternative is to have someone else do most of the work for you. For example, there are Pristine chat rooms and Pristine ESP™, Pristine's real-time scanning tool, that provide end of day lists of stocks. Any of these methods simply involve you looking at the picks and following the ones that meet your trading plan requirements. This is all in addition to the scans that are far too numerous to mention here. These scans are used to find set-ups for the next day on daily and weekly charts, as well as real-time intraday scanning with alerts. Using Pristine ESP™ alone will give you more play suggestions in whatever time frame you are in than you will ever likely need. A sample of a few of the many scans in Pristine ESP™ are shown in figure 1-1. It is opened to show the swing trader scans from the daily chart.

The third type of list would be one that you generate yourself based on the patterns you want to find. It involves scanning stocks one by one until you find a pattern that matches a strategy you want to watch the next day. This method is what the rest of this lesson will focus on.

To review a list of stocks to produce a watch list for the next day, you need to have a list of stocks to review. There are about 9,000 stocks and it would not be an easy task to look at 9,000 stocks every night. So we need to have a master list of stocks that we will look at to pick our watch list. We call this our "universe of stocks." There are two different ways to create your universe of stocks.

First, you can create a universe of stocks by compiling several indices you like to follow. If you like tech, maybe you start with the NASDAQ 100 and then add the Semi Conductor Index (there will be some overlap in many

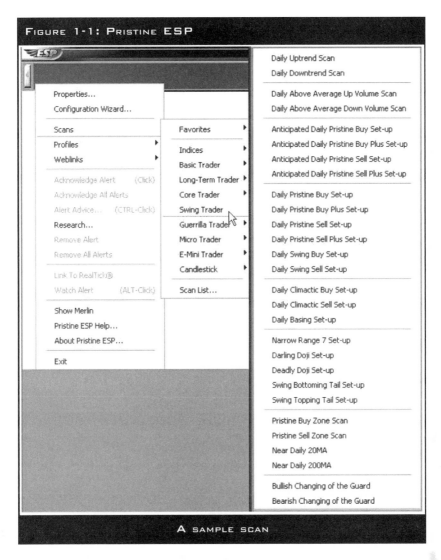

FIGURE 1-1: PRISTINE ESP

A SAMPLE SCAN

indices so your total will be less than the sum of the two indices). Maybe add the Dow, and then perhaps a few stocks you like to play, so you can add those. You may end up with 100-500 stocks in your universe.

Second, you can create a universe of stocks by starting with the entire market and then using software to scan and eliminate certain criteria. For example, if you just use two criteria such as stocks that do over one million shares a day and whose price is over $4.00, you will be down to about 400-600 total stocks, of which 200-300 will be NASDAQ stocks.

The second way, scanning, has both advantages and disadvantages. By scanning stocks to obtain your universe, you will have a different list every day. Some new stocks will join as their volume meets the requirements, some will leave as they slow up in volume. So scanning will allow you to automatically see the up and coming stocks. This is also the disadvantage because as you will have stocks entering your list that you have never seen before. Playing these often results in problems if you do not study them first.

Once you have your universe, it is simply a matter of scanning through the list every night to look for the set ups you like. Once you have some experience, you should only look at each stock for a second. If the pattern does not jump off the page at you, it is not likely to be a good one.

If you want a simple way, which takes minimal time, to manage your watch list if you are swing trading, try the following: on the weekend, review your list and look for the stocks that are defined as uptrends and downtrends. For an uptrend, look for stocks that have higher highs and higher lows, and have rising 20-and 40-period moving averages. For the best trends, look for the 20 to be above the 40 and keep a smooth, consistent distance apart. For downtrends, look for the reverse. Put these in two lists with those names. Then, every night, just look through the uptrend list for stocks that have 3-5 days down (3-5 lower highs, preferably 20-20 bars). Look through the downtrend list for 3-5 higher lows. You will then have a watch list that has the first two important components of a successful trade: a trend and a pullback.

Now that you have your list, the next lesson is about using it.

The Watch List Concept

There seems to be much confusion among new traders regarding watch lists, analyzing and entering plays. Let's review a few basic concepts.

We have already talked about how to develop a watch list. The issue now is what to do with the watch list. We put stocks on a watch list because they have formed a pattern that we recognize. They have formed a visual picture that matches a pattern we have trained our eyes to detect. This pattern is part of a strategy that we have been taught. However, the strategy has another part to it, which is when to enter the trade. The entry is almost always set to a place the stock will have a hard time crossing, or a line in the sand, so to speak.

For example, the strategy may be to play a Pristine Buy Set-up (or PBS, see Appendix A) from the daily chart over the prior day's high. The first step is to find a candidate by scanning many charts and finding a picture of a PBS that has an uptrend, a 3-5 day pullback, etc. Then, the stock goes on a watch list for the next day.

Now, here is where the problem comes in. This play should be entered long over the prior day's high. Many feel that if this is on a long watch list, it is to be played long. So, why not buy it at open and get a cheaper price? Nothing could be further from the truth. If the entry is over 32.00, let me describe how you should read the play. This stock has been falling for the last five days. It has not been able to trade over the prior day's high in five days. It has encountered selling, and that selling will likely continue. This stock is likely to fall for several more days. However, if it can trade over yesterday's high, I will play it long because it is showing the strength that may change this trend. Not just because it traded over yesterday's high, but because it did so after meeting all the criteria.

When read like that, it will stop you from thinking the wrong way. Overcoming that resistance is what makes the play work. The bigger the resistance, the stronger the stock must be to get through. It is no wonder that one trader looks at a chart and due to the resistance, sees a short. Another looks and if it breaks the resistance, sees the opportunity for a long. This is quite logical, and how you must think when you trade.

Near to this topic is the question of what plays to take. Once we meet all ten criteria for a PBS (see Appendix A), are all trades then the same? Are they all automatic buys? Do these things exist in a vacuum?

Let's say you like to fish. You have discovered an incredible lure. The lure catches fish better than anything anyone else has tried. (This is your strategy in trading talk). Now let's say you want to take your son or daughter fishing for the first time. You want to catch as many fish as possible this day. Would it matter to you if the tide was in or out? If it was 95 degrees or 40 degrees? Morning or night? From boat or shore? You may have the best lure in town, but you still look to other things to get the best fishing day. Right?

 Trading is no different. Good strategies give you the set-ups and the edge you want. Many other things will improve the odds. When following a trading plan—are the futures with you or not? Did the stock gap up? Is it extended at entry? Is the risk worth the reward? Does the direction you are playing intraday match with the long-term direction? All these things involve the study of proper entries, market internals, and experience. If you track the plays you take and make it a rule to review and evaluate, it will help you pick the best plays with better consistency.

Time Frames

The subject of time frames really involves both technical and psychological discussions. Talking about the technicals of time frames is important. Many people get confused about why a stock can look short on a 5–minute chart, long on a 15, short on a daily and long on a weekly. The best entries, of course, will have as many time frames aligned as possible. I would like to step back and discuss the bigger issues of time frames.

You may recall an earlier discussion about having an income producing and a wealth account. What is the difference? Income producing refers to an account that seeks to take money out of the market every day by executing day trades and guerrilla trades. These trades are designed to be exited the same day or one day and one night. Wealth producing refers to an account that seeks to take bigger gains out of stock movements by using swing and core trading tactics. These trades may last three to five days for a swing and weeks to months for short-and long-term cores. Some may also have a separate long-term account for an IRA or college fund.

Notice that the term "investment" is missing. I believe this term to be extinct. One can no longer close his eyes on a trade and hope that it works out. All trades have an exit point. Things can change so quickly today, as technology advances, and no company is safe from competition.

It is important to keep your income producing and wealth building accounts separate. The goals of each are different. It is difficult to hold swing positions in your day trading account. In order to let profits run, you should not overmanage the position. This will likely happen if you are looking at the position all day in your day trading account.

It is also important that you use the accounts at the proper time. Day trades occur every day, so do guerrilla tactics. Most every day, some swing trades occur due to the various sectors we look at. Core trades may not occur all the time. You should enter those only at the appropriate times based on weekly charts. Setting up these accounts properly is your key to capitalizing on market moves. Let me explain this strategy.

I had previously presented a special lecture discussing core trades and looking at some possible stocks to consider for long-term core holdings. The purpose was to be prepared to enter some long core trades so you did not have to scramble if the market suddenly looked bullish. I focused only on beaten up techs that held some support area on a weekly chart. The point was to make intelligent good-odds entries.

I identified market action that led us to be bullish for the first time in a long time. I picked one core position one week, DELL, and another the next week, YHOO. There was a list of 12 stocks we discussed as possible entries at any time, but entries may depend on individual situations. There may be different needs based on the age, available cash, and so forth.

The point of the story is this: while the market had a strong move up the first week, the first day of this move is difficult to capture in a day trading account. In this market, it is not wise to hold long position day trades all day. On most days, this leads to giving back most or all of gains. This means that only partial profits are captured in a day trading (income producing) account. But, this is the purpose of the day trading account. Those who participated and took core positions or even swing positions had something working for them the whole time. There was no need to push the day trading account. It allows for clear thinking in the day trading account because you know you are already participating in the move to the wealth building account.

Using accounts properly and clearly identifying the type of trade you are entering, along with the appropriate stop and target, is key to trading.

Your Progress as a Trader

One of the most difficult things for a new trader to measure is his own progress. Many of you may feel like you are making substantial progress, but your accounts may not show it yet... This is normal.

But how do you know where you stand? Here are some observations I have made of the levels many new traders have passed on their way to becoming successful traders.

You may be someone, who has had some great successes, only to give it all back quickly. Trying desperately for those successes to return, you got frustrated and lost money. You just could not seem to find the groove you once had. You increased your share size and started keeping more overnights to get the home run to get you back to even. Eventually, your account started draining and you needed that home run more than ever. Of course, it never came.

Or you may be at the next stage. You are in a trading room. Maybe you have had a seminar or two. You see the plays. You see the strategies. You are excited because you see the trades work right in front of you. It's not like reading about someone's past conquests in a book, you are seeing the strategies in play, but you are having one of several problems. You just can't pull the trigger on a play. You might be trying, but are always just a little too late, so you either chase it to your detriment or you miss the play. Or, you seem to always pick the loser. You pick it first and then are gun shy the rest of the day. Or you might get the winner and sell it fast only to watch the room go on to hold it for a big winner. This is a common phase. You have to ask, how did some of the others get beyond this, why or how did they get in the play?

Alternatively, you may fall into another category. You are really starting to feel good. You are getting in the plays and starting to hold some winners. You are developing a real sense for getting out of the losers just in the nick of time. You are starting to grow your account. But, just then, you find a mistake comes along. It takes you back to where you were. Hmmmm, you say, you won't do that again. You don't. But, low and behold, another mistake comes along—a different one, but with the same result. However, you are getting smarter now and you keep eliminating those mistakes. If you do, you are one of the ones who make it to the next step. If not, you spend a long time in this phase trying to rid yourself of mistakes, but just can't do it. Eventually you will, but it becomes a race between getting these final touches down and making your account last.

Finally, those who make it get a feeling of calm in the morning. While you always have enjoyed trading, it is now relaxing rather than nerve racking. You look back on all those rules you learned and realized they were all that was needed. You just needed to know how to follow them. You just needed to really get it right the second time. Experience has

29

come in and developed your sense of art for trading. Where all the technical analysis in the world tells you a stock will hold at this support level, you get a sense that it will not, so you are ready to get out quickly, and it saves you. You take a loss on a good trade in stride and take the play again the next time it comes up because it was a good play.

How long does it take to get through this process? Many time estimates have been given. I believe my experience is typical of many. My feeling of calm came over me after about 9 to 11 months of trading full time. It is hard to say; everyone is different. So what do you do to get through these steps? Well, if you are here reading this, you are already through the first step. You are getting training in a system and a discipline. It won't guarantee success, but it will almost guarantee failure if you don't get the help, or at least ensure a long learning period that takes lots of capital.

If you are in the second phase, where you just can't get involved or make the plays work for you, you need to do several things. Attend a trading seminar to learn the basics in a classroom fashion. Follow an online trading room closely and absorb what is being done. Watch for a while, paper trade, and finally trade small shares. Start with risk amounts of $50, then move to $100, $150, $250, etc., only upon successful trading at each new level of risk. Learn and build confidence without burning through cash.

Develop a trading plan and play only the stocks that fall into your plan. When you play them, make up your mind to play them. Get in first, sell in stages where you have determined to, and follow your stops. You must be able to trust yourself first. You must track your trades, using a strategy tracking spreadsheet. Eliminate mistakes; track all the data regarding your trades and follow a plan.

If you pick losing plays all the time and just can't figure out why, consider that it may not be bad luck. Perhaps you have a mindset for picking what you consider to be the safest play at a calmer time of day that is easier to enter. But consider also, maybe things are not as they seem. Is this really safer, once the market is quiet, once people are letting you buy the stock?

Think about it. You may be attracting plays that are destined to lose. Many plays that require early entries during hectic market times admittedly are anything but calming but can be among the most successful.

I always want to promote reducing risk as much as possible in trading, though some of you may be too far on the other extreme. Recognize trading has inherent risks and some of them cannot be eliminated. A famous entrepreneur once said: "Not many people will pay to see a high wire act where the tight rope is only one foot off the ground.... why? Because there is no risk, and without risk, there can be no reward...."

If you have made it to the next stage, have realized some rewards, and are doing well but just can't get the account up due to a few problems, consider this analogy taken from the great American sport of baseball. Consider a batter that hits .333 for any season can name his price in baseball. Anyone who does this year after year will be Hall of Fame material and be among the highest paid athletes on the planet. Consider that a batter who hits .250 will be sent back to the minors that year unless he has a great glove, or is a pitcher. Now consider this. The difference between .333 and .250 is one hit in three times at bat versus one hit in four times at bat. That means that for every 12 times at bat, the superstar gets one more hit than the minor leaguer. Consider how many hits often are the result of a ball passing just inches from a defender's glove, a defender who could have been playing one step out of place. Consider how many outs were the result of hitting a line drive shot that happened to be right in a defenders glove, one who never even saw the ball coming.

What is the point? Just this. Sometimes you are very close to being successful, but that 1 in 12 hit is eluding you. If you had a few bad trades, maybe you have eliminated them. Maybe you were very close to not being in those trades. You just need to fine tune, don't lose focus, and let your senses develop. *The plans and rules keep you in the game while you are learning and keep you in for the long term.*

Remember that a seminar, or any kind of instruction, no matter how excellent, is only information. The process of taking that information and translating it to a workable system demands hard work, experience, and discipline on your part. Most people do not understand this, and of those who do understand, few are actually willing to commit the hard work. Of those, even fewer have the needed discipline.

The hardest thing for me, of course, is to try to communicate all of this to you. This is not an easy profession. Many of those who learned to trade in the late 1990s are gone. Many fooled themselves. They mistook learning a difficult profession with just riding a bull market. They could be sloppy and it would not matter. It was just a matter of time before the stock came back. Many traders never even knew how to short. Why would they? The market will never go down.

Since then we have experienced a record fall, a substantial move up, and lots of sideways action. Only those who are well educated have played these moves correctly. Those learning now are getting all the tools, all the tactics, and waging battle at a time that will benefit them for the rest of their lives.

Chapter 2
Lessons on Some Basics

What Market Is That Again?

The market is full of terms like the Spoos, the futures, the Dow, the e-minis, the HOLDRS, the cash market. If you are new to trading, hearing all these terms may be enough to make your head spin. All you wanted to know was how the market was doing. What do all these terms mean?

Well, let's start from the top. The "market" generally means the whole stock market. There are three main exchanges that trade the vast majority of all stocks. They are the New York Stock Exchange (NYSE), the NASDAQ Stock Exchange, and the American Stock Exchange (AMEX). While the numbers change, the NASDAQ currently is the largest with about 3,300 stocks trading. The NYSE is next with about 2,700, and the AMEX last with about 800.

However, it is more common to view the market through the eyes of an index. This is a list of the larger key stocks that are thought to be representative of the market itself. Some indices you might have heard of are the S&P 500, the NASDAQ 100, and the Dow Industrials (Dow).

The S&P 500 is widely regarded as the best single gauge of the U.S. equities market. It is a representative sample of 500 leading companies in leading industries of the U.S. economy. Although the S&P 500 focuses on the large-cap segment of the market, with over 80 percent coverage of U.S. equities, it is also an ideal proxy for the total market. To view the actual price and chart of the S&P 500, you put in the symbol for the cash index. For example, on Realtick, that symbol is $INX.X.

The NASDAQ-100 index includes 100 of the largest domestic and international non-financial companies listed on the NASDAQ stock market based on market capitalization. Index reflects companies across major industry groups including computer hardware and software, telecommunications, retail/wholesale trade, and biotechnology. To view the actual price and chart of the NASDAQ 100, you put in the symbol for the cash index. For example, on Realtick that symbol is $NDX.X.

The Dow is an index of only 30 stocks, thought to be a cross section of our entire market. It often is used as the representative of the U.S. market globally. It is maintained and reviewed by editors of *The Wall Street Journal*. For the sake of continuity, composition changes are rare and generally occur only after corporate acquisitions or other dramatic shifts in a component's core business. To view the actual price and chart of the Dow, you put in the symbol for the cash index. For example, on Realtick, that symbol is $DJI.

Note that there can be overlap. Intel Corporation (INTC), for example, is in the NASDAQ 100, S&P 500, and the Dow.

There are also HOLDRS and ETFs, which often are confused. HOLDRS (spelled correctly even though it is pronounced as 'holders') is an acronym for Holding Company Depositary Receipts and are service marks of Merrill Lynch & Co., Inc. They are securities that represent an investor's ownership in the common stock or American Depositary Receipts of specified companies in a particular industry, sector, or group. In other words, they are traded like a single stock but in most cases represent ownership in several stocks in a sector. Common HOLDRS traders use BBH for the Biotech sector and HHH for the Internet sector.

ETF is an acronym for Exchange Traded Fund. Each ETF is a basket of securities designed to track an index (stock or bond, stock industry sector, or international stock), yet trades like a single stock. There are more than 120 ETFs, and the most commonly used are the QQQ, SPY, and DIA. These are the ETFs for the NASDAQ 100, S&P 500, and Dow Industrials.

In addition to the above, there are also futures. A futures contract is an obligation to receive or deliver a commodity or financial instrument sometime in the future, but at a price that's agreed upon today. People commonly think of futures in corn and pork bellies. But futures have also been developed for financial markets. As you might guess, there are futures for the NASDAQ 100, S&P 500, and the Dow. To view, these must be permissioned to receive futures quotes (talk to your broker). Symbols on Realtick during this timeframe were /NDM4, /SPM4, and /ZDU4, respectively (the S&P Futures is the one that carries the nickname 'Spoos'). Note, the last two characters 'M4' represent the month and year of the future and change every quarter.

E-Minis

The most popular financial futures contracts were set up as new trading instruments by reducing their size. This set up is a series of products known as the e-minis. They are available for the NASDAQ 100, S&P 500, and the Dow. Their symbols are /NQM4, /ESM4, and /YMM4 respectively. They are popular due to the reduced size and requirements.

So, how many ways could you view the S&P 500? Well, there is the cash index ($INX.X), the Exchange Traded Fund (SPY), the future (/SPM4), the E-mini future (/ESM4). Is there any difference in the chart patterns? Well, they are all tied to the same underlying instrument, the price action of the S&P 500. So, at the end of the day, the chart patterns all will be similar. However, depending on what is happening in the market, the intraday price action may vary slightly as one of these may begin to move ahead of the others. Figure 2-1 shows four different ways to view the S&P.

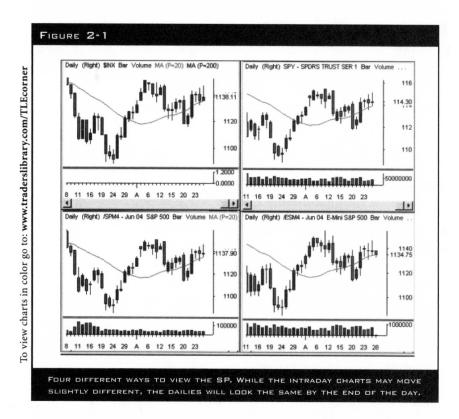

FIGURE 2-1

FOUR DIFFERENT WAYS TO VIEW THE SP. WHILE THE INTRADAY CHARTS MAY MOVE SLIGHTLY DIFFERENT, THE DAILIES WILL LOOK THE SAME BY THE END OF THE DAY.

So when you hear someone say 'the market,' they likely are referring to whatever they last discussed, or they may be just using the term in a generic way to describe the action of all stocks. There often will be very different patterns when you compare the NASDAQ to the S&P 500, or any other individual sector. Sometimes they will look similar. However, whatever instrument you use to view the S&P 500, be it the cash index, the ETF, the futures ('Spoos') or the E-minis, they will look similar at the end of the day because they are all viewing the same instrument, that same basket of 500 stocks.

I hope this helps to clarify some of the terms and gives you a better idea of what you want to be looking at.

Looking at the Big Picture

I have often said that no one knows with any certainty the long-term direction or duration of the stock market. The longer the time frame, the less certainty there is. Even on a day-to-day basis, there is no certainty. We often look to certain patterns to reproduce themselves, but news events, earnings, company announcements, upgrades, and downgrades always make anticipation of market moves a risky business. If you think the stock market will always go up, look at the last few years. Years of profits can be taken away in 18 months. What if it takes 40 years to return to those levels? At that time, they can once again say that the trend is always up, but will that be meaningful to you? Look at Japan over the last 20 years. Nothing can be taken for granted.

So why do we study the pattern? What can we gain if all the study in the world still falls short of any kind of certainty? There are very valid reasons to keep an eye on the direction of the market and individual stocks.

First of all, while even the short term (three to five day) outlook cannot be predicted, certain patterns do give us the low risk entries to strategies we use. Take for example a market or a stock that has been in an uptrend (we can always define and find the trend by looking at charts and the history of prior price action) and pulls back for a few days to an area of support. Then on that day, it gets the strength to close over its open price. Whether you play the market or a particular stock that shows the same pattern (and many will), this often draws a line in the sand where we can play strategies, knowing that the current day's low is the support upon which we are relying. That will be the stop for the play. The target usually will be far larger than the stop, as it looks to challenge or exceed prior highs when in a trend. Patterns often do repeat, like on the chart in figure 2-2, a daily chart for Zimmer Holdings.

Often, traders overreact to the moves a stock may have on a smaller time frame and forget that patience is necessary to play the bigger time frame. When playing the daily chart, it is often the case that a stock makes a

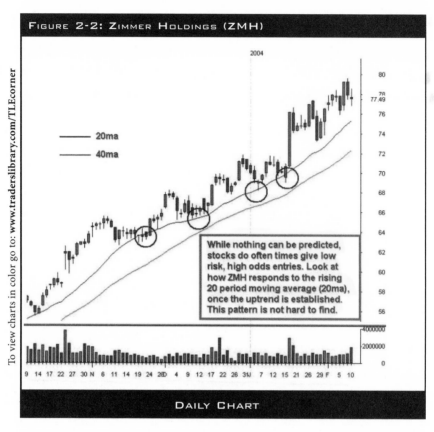

FIGURE 2-2: ZIMMER HOLDINGS (ZMH)

2004

—— 20ma

—— 40ma

While nothing can be predicted, stocks do often times give low risk, high odds entries. Look at how ZMH responds to the rising 20 period moving average (20ma), once the uptrend is established. This pattern is not hard to find.

DAILY CHART

beautiful move, but the trader had sold the stock long ago. Why? The trader sold because he forgot that he was playing the daily chart, and overreacted to intraday moves. He was shaken out even though the proper time frame showed no reason to sell. If you want the bigger moves on the daily chart, you may have to live through some pullbacks intraday.

Second, it can be important to know exactly what stage the market is in, as shown in the daily chart for CIT Group (Figure 2-3). You'll find that different strategies have varying degrees of success depending on where the market is in a bigger time frame. For example, in a strong uptrending market, you will find that basing patterns frequently are broken to the upside forming a stair step pattern. This is a strong pattern in a strong market. However, the same trader who continues to use this pattern

FIGURE 2-3: CIT GROUP (CIT)

2004

—— 20ma
—— 40ma

Stage Two Uptrend

Again, look at the big picture. If you are playing the bigger time frame, the daily chart in this case, how would you do if you simply bought every time that CIT entered the PBZ and sold new highs?

9 14 17 22 27 30 N 6 11 14 19 24 28 D 4 9 12 17 22 26 31 J 7 12 15 21 26 29 F 5 10

DAILY CHART

To view charts in color go to: www.traderslibrary.com/TLEcorner

without recognizing that the market has now lost momentum and is in a basing phase will not have the same success. Traders will find that break-outs do not carry as far or they start to fail and become losses.

Let me provide a real life example. At a recent mentorship, a student arrived who had been very successful over the prior six months, but was having great trouble the last few weeks. He was a good student who had a good trading plan and liked to play basing stocks. He had a great feeling of success after playing basing stocks in a market that was moving strongly in one direction. He became a little complacent and did not continue to track his results and strategies. He did not notice that his favorite play was no longer providing profits. When asked, he felt that his basic strategy was still his most successful, even over the prior few weeks. Looking deeper, it was revealed that this was not an accurate statement based on his trading record. He felt it to be true, because he remembered only the success of that strategy. Many of us do this.

How could the trader have avoided this? He needs to understand his strategy and know when it is best suited for the current market. Second, he should keep an eye on major trends in the market and any change in trend to reevaluate the strategies that he is currently using to avoid the problem. Also, if he continues to track his results and strategies, he'll notice the change in success rates of the different strategies he uses as the market changes. I don't mean just long or short. I mean which particular strategy to be used when you are long and how aggressive to be with the targets. Is it appropriate to go for new highs or 40 percent retracements? Is it best not to trade that time frame at all based on the strategies in your trading plan?

So how does a new trader begin to understand the basics of the current market trend? Let me give you a few guidelines that hold true at any experience level. Moving averages are always a good guide for establishing the current trend. Are the 20ma and 40ma rising or falling? Is the price above or below the 200ma? Is the 20ma above the 40ma? Are we in a pattern of higher highs and higher lows or are they starting to even off, showing the potential for a base to form? Are the Wide Range Bars (WRBs) green or red, and do they hold their moves or are they reversed?

Many traders like to be market gurus and make bold predictions regarding the market. I think it is a wiser choice to follow a plan, play proven strategies, and always keep a close eye on what the market has done to help you determine your best course of action in the future. Have separate accounts for wealth building (swing and core positions) and for income producing (day trading and guerrilla positions) so you can cash in on the bigger moves.

A Guide to Protective Stop Losses

Protective stop losses. You have read about them. You have been lectured about them. You still don't use them properly. What do you do? The purpose of this lesson is to go into more detail and say more than just "you must use them." I will try to explain why you may not be using them properly, and give suggestions for new ways to use them.

Let's get a few facts out first. Fact number one: most traders do not make it in the long term, especially those who do not get training. Fact number two: most traders who fail do so due to not following their stops. Fact number three: your goal is to get to the point where you follow stops like a reflex, just like you would jump out of the way of a speeding car. There is no in between. Either you follow them or you don't. I will offer suggestions to reach this goal, but they are not substitutes for this goal. You must accept that you have a flaw and that it needs to be fixed.

What is a stop loss? It is a line in the sand, right? A spot which is chosen to represent the maximum loss on a trade? Not completely. Most people don't realize that the stop loss comes from the chart. Depending on the play, some may have tight stops and some may be wide. You really need to know the stop first, so you can play the right number of shares so your maximum loss on a trade is within the limits you have set in your trading plan You can't change the stop because that would violate the integrity of the play. You can adjust your share size to make the potential loss within your limits. You can pass on the play if it does not fit into your plan. You may not realize it, but this is the first step in following your stop. Have a trade and share size you can live with.

Consider trader Jane. Once upon a time she bought a stock as it broke out from an all-afternoon long base. Her stop was below the low of the base. The stock started up, and then pulled back to the base. Then the stock fell below the base, then below the stop. In disbelief, Jane just froze. This was a perfect set up; it just couldn't fail! Now the stock really plummets. She can't sell now; obviously, it can't go any lower. She doesn't want to sell at the low of the day. So she hangs on. The stock starts to come back. It rallies back to the base, then back above. It turns out to be a big winner.

This is a problem for Jane. In my book *Tools and Tactics for the Master Day Trader*, I call this "winning the wrong way." It does not matter how many times Jane now loses money by violating her stops. She will always remember this one winner. That is the way the mind works, it remembers what it wants. In the Pristine Method® trading room, we are big on teaching the tracking of trades and printing charts and identifying mistakes. By doing this you would know that, most of the time, violating a stop results in more losses. Jane may go on violating stops because she remembers only that one time—the one time her loser became a winner.

Consider trader John. Maybe you can relate to his story. He goes long on a stock. It never goes quite right. The futures start slipping. His stock hits his stop. He does not sell it because he feels he is an experienced trader and his stock deserves a little more room. After all, his stock is holding up well, it is just the futures that have slipped. If they come back, surely his stock will do well. If he sells now, it is likely to come shooting back. And because he is in the trade, it is worth a little more investment to give it a chance. Does this sound familiar? The stock does not come back much, and John starts looking at his stop. He realizes that his stop was awfully tight, and just a little bit lower is a major area of support. So he makes that his new stop. Of course, that stop comes close, and he now looks and realizes that the low of the day is not far below, and that will be solid support. That will be the final stop.

Of course, as that stop gets violated, John starts thinking that he can't sell it now: it can't get any lower, and it is due to bounce. Besides, the daily chart has support in this area. Finally, in some truly sad situations, John may start looking up the fundamentals of the company. He has taken a scalp off of a five-minute chart and now has an investment. How did this happen? Does any of this sound familiar? Looking back, that original stop was not such a bad idea.

So what do we do? First, as we have discussed previously, have a trading plan. You need to have outlined how many shares you can trade with a stop loss at a certain point. This strategy ensures that you are trading with a share size that allows you to take a loss when needed.

Second, have your plan and all of your rules in writing. Your plan should be very specific. It should be written as a promise to yourself. Your mind responds differently to the written word. It truly does. You must write and review your rules and keep a top 10 list every week. If your rule is simply to always follow stops, but it is not working, try this:

1. I will sell all of my position at my written stop loss every time.

2. If I am too foolish to do the above, I promise I will sell half of my position.

3. I will then sell the back half of my position at the next support level that is violated.

4. If I am too foolish to do the above, I will sell the last half at the low of the day.

5. If I am too foolish to do the above, I will sell the last half at the end of the day.

6. If I am too foolish to do the above, I will quit trading.

By selling half, it lets you get into the habit of doing what is right, while appeasing the terrible place in your mind that does not want to be a loser. You will find it easier to sell half. Once you sell half, your mind will start thinking properly again. If you cannot get rid of the back half, you must sell by the end of the day. Never hold a loser overnight. That is a career stopper.

In summary, have a trading plan. Define what you are allowed to lose on a trade. Define what your share size can be on a trade. Define what your goals are so your subconscious knows what being a loser is. If you are three for seven in winning trades but you made money, are you a loser? Write your rules and learn to follow them. Sell half for now if you can't sell it all. You must get to the point where stops are automatic and reflexive. Finally, never, never take home a loser.

Always remember, that there are many people who held positions from $250.00 all the way to $10.00 or lower over the last three years. Did people intend to do this? Did they use plays with $240.00 stops? Of course not. Most of them entered a day trade with a tight stop, and did not honor the stop when it hit. Once that happens, it becomes harder and harder to sell at any level. This is why we call the stop an 'insurance policy.' Do not ever let this happen to you. If the market falls for the next 12 months, where will you be exiting your swings? Are you sure about that?

Trading the First Half Hour

A large number of the questions I receive often revolve around trading the first 30 minutes of the day. This only stands to reason as the opening half hour usually provides plenty of volatility. The large amount of volume that comes during this period means that a trader must be very organized and have his system functioning properly. This time period often provides major moves for many stocks. Depending on the day, the majority of the move and volume may come to the stock during this opening half-hour. The purpose of this lesson is to provide you with some basic information to help you get organized during this time.

The open can be very profitable if played correctly. This is where guerrilla tactics and other strategies that utilize gaps in the opening of stocks come into play. A few things need to be understood first. First, the open often has very little to do with the rest of the day. Overnight, orders are being filled, market makers are positioning to capitalize on the morning, and trading during this time can be very whippy. It usually is a riskier time to enter longer-term positions. So the first rule is to stick to strategies that are designed for the opening, such as guerrilla tactics, gap strategies, and intraday tactics.

Understand that the saying "amatures open the market and profession-als close the market" has some truth to it. It often is riskier using swing type entries that occur during the first 30 minutes. Using support and resistance (see Chapter 5) and the ten o'clock Reversal Time (discussed later on page 59) can be the source of many good plays. Don't be on the wrong side of these.

The second important rule is to be very organized. Traders often ask how it is possible to follow so many stocks during the opening minutes and still make intelligent plays. The truth is that though there may be many stocks on your watch list, many stocks on the gap list, and many stocks in the news, you simply cannot follow all of these during the opening minutes. Pick your favorites from your watch list and from the gap list. If you are going to play early, focus hard on just a few. Decide ahead of time what the stock must do for you to take a play. Don't chase anything you miss during the opening.

One tip to help you follow multiple stocks is to have an area set up on your page with several 5- or 2- minute charts. Or, you could also set up an opening page that consists largely of 5- or 2- minute charts. These charts are very helpful in determining at a glance how all the stocks in which you have an interest are acting. However, you will still have to pick your favorites to watch during the opening minutes. If you ever had the feeling of constantly flipping from one stock to the next and always being behind the play and never making a good entry, this may be your prob-lem. You will be much better off if you pick a few favorites and follow them for the exact entry that you are seeking.

The third rule is to make sure that your system is working properly and can handle the high volume demands of the opening minutes. Many people who have a hard time entering plays during the open do not even realize that they may be behind and seeing ghosts on their screen. Here are a few tips. Understand what is the most reliable source of data on your system. For example, if you're using Realtick, a time and sales win-dow or a chart usually will show the most accurate data. Next comes the

Level One screen, which is the top part of your Level Two screen. The slowest and the least accurate will be the Level Two screen itself. So if there is a conflict between any of these prices, understand that trading may be very risky.

If you are having serious speed problems in the morning, consider setting up a page just to handle the opening minutes. This page should contain minimal items. Use just what you need to view a few stocks and make a trade if needed. You could have just one Level Two screen, a time and sales window, and a handful of 2- or 5-minute charts, including a chart of the futures and the TRIN (the trader's index). Set this page to open automatically. In case of a lock up, you will go to this page on restart, rather than the page that caused the lock up.

If you have access to more than one computer, consider using your fastest computer for trading and dedicate it to your trading software. If you have access to more than one high-speed Internet connection, consider dedicating your fastest connection directly to your trading computer. You can network any other computers to your secondary Internet connection.

Many people ask if they should even try to trade the first 30 minutes because of the evil market makers and the volatile moves. If you are a trader, the answer is that anything can be profitable if you understand how it trades. The first 30 minutes can be the best time of the day.

Fundamental vs. Technical

Ever since the first mathematician plotted some sort of graph that compared price to time, there has been a debate about whether price patterns or the basics of the underlying security are better predictors of price movement.

Investors who believe that fundamentals are the primary reason to buy and sell stock are relying on the underlying economics of the business itself, the industry, and the economy as a whole. They look to things like the balance sheet of the company, earnings reports, and raw material supply. They look at the experience and depth of the company's management. They look at economists' outlook for the industry. They look at the prime rate and if the government is likely to cut rates. They tend to hold for a longer term, primarily because the things on which they are basing their decisions do not change overnight. Most fundamentalists would agree that they would not buy AMZN in the morning and sell it in the afternoon based on fundamental reasons.

Traders who believe that technical analysis is the primary reason to buy and sell stocks are relying on three beliefs. Technical traders, or technicians, believe that the price is a total reflection of all forces in the market, and this includes all economic and fundamental information. They believe that prices move in trends and are repetitive, sometimes in a predictable way. They believe that people's emotions are a large driving force in prices, and these patterns can be seen in charts. Technicians will hold stocks for a variety of time periods, from a small part of the day to weeks or months. However, they do not believe in the buy and hold philosophy.

I have given you a quick summary of both approaches. However, I am not going to deceive you. I am going to show you why I believe the technical approach to be the superior one. When I started, I went through this same dilemma, as I am sure many of you have, believing that only fundamentals are the way to buy and sell stocks. Later, I believed that only technical analysis was the way to go. Usually, when dilemmas like this hit, we land somewhere in the middle. However, for me this is not the case. I believe technical analysis is the best and only buy and sell indicator.

Notice above that I used the term "investor" for the fundamentalist, and the term "trader" for the technician. This is a reflection of the longer-term outlook you must have when using fundamentals. Due to the many changing things in the market place, we believe that the concept of 'buy and hold' no longer is valid. There are several reasons, but consider the following. Years ago the major companies were more industrial. They had big plants that required big start-up costs. No one could open a competitor to General Motors overnight. It took huge resources. Today, many of the biggest companies are high tech, producing computers, related devices, and software. This technology changes quickly and almost anyone can enter the field with a good idea and some creativity. It is the concept that two kids in a garage can bring a company to its knees

Was there money to be made in Internet companies in the 1990's? There were stocks that literally went from one dollar to hundreds in some cases. They did this on no earnings, no earnings predictions for next year, and on borrowed money. No fundamentalist could justify purchases in most of these. Yet technicians had a field day.

Even if you do believe that fundamentals should figure into the equation, how do you handle the realization that we really don't know what the fundamentals are? The Enron debacle has opened the eyes of many investors to what has always been the case. Companies can twist things any way they like. What information can you believe?

Despite belief to the contrary, it is the technical trader who has less risk than the fundamental investor. In all things, we can be more certain of what will happen tomorrow than we can of what will happen next year. Technical traders sell losing positions as part of their philosophy. Fundamental investors hold under the belief that all is well until the fundamentals that were the basis for their entry change. It brings up an interesting question that many fundamentalists have a hard time answering. Just when do you enter a stock based on fundamentals? When do you take profit? When do you cut your losses and move on? The answers to these questions usually are random numbers, or they simply do not exist.

I believe in making decisions from charts. My core trades, which are designed to last weeks to months, may be long term, but still get their primary buy and sell signals from charts. You will find that fundamental information usually is reflected in price changes in the stock before it is reported as a fundamental change. It is not that technicians believe that fundamentals are wrong; it is simply that we believe they already are built into the charts.

News You Can Use?

So, you have decided to be a day trader. What is the first step (and often last) for the new day traders? Why, turn on CNBC and wait for the news, of course (don't deny it, you have been there). Then when you hear the late breaking real-time news, you buy good news (or sell short bad news) in an attempt to beat the other 8 million listeners. Sound like a winning plan?

After realizing that this is a hit or miss approach, you decide to fire up the real real-time news service. Of course, at this point, it hasn't dawned on you. It is not just the fact that you are not really beating anyone to the news. You begin to realize that even if you do have the news first, what do you do with it?

Have you ever heard of a stock gapping up big on fantastic earnings, then selling off for two weeks? We have all seen it: good news reacted to in a negative way and bad news reacted to in a positive way. Or, good news reacted to in such a positive way that the stock gaps so far you are not sure what to do. How do you make sense of all this?

First of all, you may just want to turn off the news. Yes, that is correct. You can track the stocks that are in the news for your watch list if you like. However, you can skip the part about researching the news. This does not sit well with many traders. They believe it is their job to research these things. The truth is that you cannot. We play people's reactions to the news, not our personal view of what the news is. We do this by looking at charts.

Next are some examples. Two of them resulted in plays. Look at what happened compared to the news. These three were picked because they all solicited a strong view from many traders, even by email. "Did you know that xyz had bad news today and you are playing it long?!"

Below is a chart of McDonalds (Figure 2-4). The day in question is December 24, 2003. You may remember the mad cow scare that day. All fast food restaurants gapped down, and the overwhelming consensus was (even CNBC told me this) that this scare is the end of the American hamburger. It would be a no-brainer to short these stocks, as they are certain to fall more.

Well, if they are certain to fall more, why didn't they open at that lower price? You see, there are no gifts. The news was out and was digested (no pun intended) by the public. What the stock does after that is not a function of good or bad news. It opens at equilibrium—and then the move can be in either direction. This chart pattern (without any concern for the news) was bearish, but it did not form a pattern that we recognize as a trade. No play was made, though there were possibilities for intraday plays once the trend was set. Notice how long the bad news continued

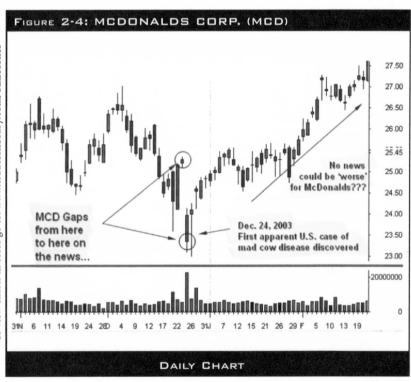

to hurt the stock. Why did it go up? Who knows? Well, there were many commentators and analysts who told us the answer after the close. One of the stories was that the shock sent beef prices tumbling, which would reduce the operating costs of fast food restaurants. Now why didn't I think of that?

Next, a daily chart for Marathon Oil (Figure 2-5): here, there was little chance for failure.

The company was doing a secondary offering or something similar. On the morning in question, they actually came out and priced the stock below the current price (even below where it opened). Certainly, this stock had to go down further. Well, this time, the chart showed a pattern of a guerrilla tactic known as a "Gap and Snap" play. Pristine played this one, buying shortly after the open as a swing trade. How could a stock go

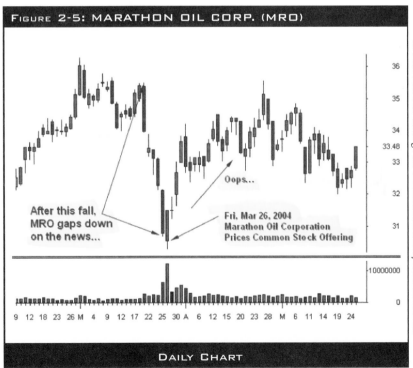

FIGURE 2-5: MARATHON OIL CORP. (MRO)

After this fall, MRO gaps down on the news...

Oops...

Fri, Mar 26, 2004
Marathon Oil Corporation
Prices Common Stock Offering

DAILY CHART

To view charts in color go to: www.traderslibrary.com/TLEcorner

up in this situation? Read the McDonalds paragraph on the prior page. All the answers are the same. Even I don't understand enough about secondary stock offerings to try to explain it. Or, if I do understand, it is not worth explaining. That is the point. The best way to play this was to have no knowledge of the actual news, just to know that the stock was gapping to find the play.

Finally, here is a recent play on Delta Airlines (Figure 2-6). This is one of my favorites because we have our friends, the analysts, coming in to help us determine when to buy and sell stocks.

On May 10, the big news posted that Delta may have to file for bankruptcy. Is the stock worthless? Or is it worth asset value? That day, the stock did not go below $4.53. On the next day, we have a revision of Delta Airlines' outlook to negative. The day after that, Moody's decides

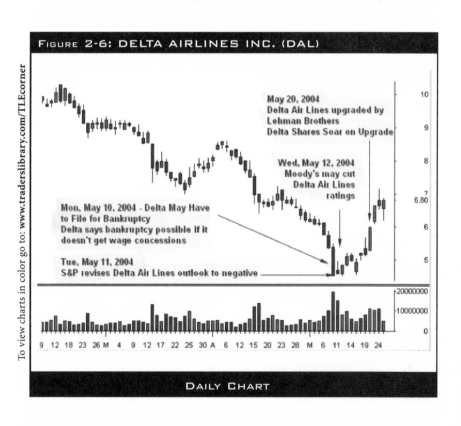

it may cut Delta's ratings. The stock talks bankruptcy, and then analysts downgrade it. Do we need to pay analysts for this keen information and insight? Note the stock has never traded under the low set on May 10, the day the news of bankruptcy was released. Notice the volume that came in on that day. Notice that this volume came in after the stock already dropped 66 percent in four months. Now, Mr. Analyst, you are downgrading the stock? Where were you during this huge fall? Waiting for the company to tell us they are in trouble? This stock was played as a swing long by Pristine on May 12 at $4.67.

Note the last news item on May 20. DAL gets upgraded. Most swing traders come home to find the stock upgraded, and at $6.02. This means it has rallied 33 percent off of the lows.

News will move stocks. It can be a means of finding stocks to watch and see if any technical patterns form. Do not get caught up in the game of trying to make trades based on your analyses of the news. For more information on how news is used in trading, see the following lesson.

News and Your Trading

As we've discussed, news is always a controversial topic. Good traders may disagree about the extent to which they use news in their trading. Fundamental traders may use news heavily. Purely technical traders may not use it at all.

I want to walk you through a little exercise I do at my Mentorships. I usually ask how many people have real-time news. Typically about half the students raise their hands. I then tell them they are wrong, which usually gets funny looks. I then explain that the only real time news occurs in a closed office, when the accountant tells the CEO that they are in trouble. Everything after that is old news. By the time the appropriate people in the company are told, memos are typed, plans are made, families and friends are told, a press release is put together, and damage control people are brought in... well, you get the idea.

We see this every day in the chart. A stock drops for two days, or has crashed during the last hour of trading. News is then released the next morning. Were those all just good traders getting out? Well, if they use charts, the likely answer is, "yes." In the beginning, people who have heard something are getting out.

There is no doubt that news moves stocks and markets. Earnings, interest rate adjustments, sentiment numbers, acquisitions, and CEOs leaving all make for moves. The question is, can you profit by playing the news after it is released?

Try the following exercise. Let's say you are sitting at your trading computer after hours when company XYZ is going to release earnings. You have a super news service that will get you the earnings number substantially before CNBC gives it. Let's say it is even early enough to make a trade. You want to go long or short depending on the earnings. Ready? Earnings are up 25 percent over last year, the biggest increase ever for company XYZ. So what button do you hit, Buy or Short? Buy, you say? What if earnings were expected to be up by 40 percent? This would be built into the price, and 25 percent may be a disappointment.

Many of you realized that already. So let's say you are there again, ready to trade the announcement. This time you are armed with knowledge that expectations were for 22 percent, and they did 25 percent, so they beat the number. Now do you buy? If you buy now, what if I told you there was a whisper number, an expectation that is not as published, but built into the price by the analysts? Does your buy still sound like a buy?

So you were aware of that. Let's get the facts you want to hear. The expectations are for 18 cents, the whisper number is for 21 cents, and now the earnings come out at 25 cents. Now it must be a buy, right? Well, maybe not. What if the daily chart showed a strong 8-day rally into the announcement? There may not be news good enough to stem the tide of sellers. This is a typical buy the rumor and sell the news scenario.

What if a stock gaps up $3.00 in the morning on good news? Let's forget the role of market makers for a minute and their need to exaggerate gaps. Just consider a stock's value, if there is such a term. If it is up on $3.00 on real good news, should it head higher or lower? The truth is that it is neutral (if you ignore market makers). After all, the news has been digested by all that are going to buy or sell it, and all the bids and offers are placed, the stock has opened $3.00 to the plus. This is the equilibrium point—the spot where all buyers and sellers at that moment have decided the stock could open. Could there be buyers waiting to buy on a dip? Could there be sellers waiting to sell on a rally? Of course. However, we do not know which—that is the issue.

There are appropriate uses of news. If a stock is gapping up, it is good to know if it was acquired for cash. It won't be moving much if it was. It is also good to know if an analyst upgrade moved a stock that already was up substantially. They often have other motives for talking up a stock; so, it is nice, but not necessary to know. Scalpers can play the rush into news for small moves if the news is timely. Some traders have learned to fade news, letting good news run a stock up, and shorting the fall. However, the trader is playing the chart for a scalp set-up. The real value of news is that it can serve as a big watch list. Start to follow it because it made the news, but play it based on the chart patterns that you have learned to play. Technicals can confirm the news you hear.

Remember, as traders, we don't trade stocks, we trade people. We don't trade news; we trade the reaction to news. Keep this in perspective and follow your trading rules.

Are You Still Investing?

Are you still investing? Should you be? Well, it may just be our choice of words, but we believe the term "investing" is no longer a valid term. Now, don't get me wrong. We firmly believe in being diversified over different times, and that includes the longer term. We have core positions that theoretically could last forever. What is the difference between a long term core position and investing? Simple. Our core trades always will be managed and sold if they do not maintain certain criteria on the period chosen. Most people look at investing as a commitment for life, or simply have no plans on how to manage. (Right now, do you know what you would sell for profit or take a loss on any of your investments?). We call investing the "Rip Van Winkle" play. Go to sleep for 20 years and when you wake up, hope all is well.

Depending on how active you are, you may hold for weeks to months taking trades based on the weekly chart or, just for several days based on the daily chart. It is not unlikely for a stock to be up 20 percent for the year, and actually make a 20 percent or more move several times on the daily charts. Rally, then pull back. Look at the daily chart for Yahoo (Figure 2-7), over just a few months. This is not an unusual occurrence.

You can see that a nearly perfect bullish move has been erased. Even with the best of all entries, all gains are gone. A safer entry, such as buying the breakout rather than the Pristine Buy Set-up (see Appendix A) on the daily chart would mean that you are now losing money.

 By using the daily chart to enter and exit, you would be in and out on the way up, and out at the top. You would also be making money on the last couple drops on the way down. You may have lost on one long play at the top, but you would have preserved all of the moves on prior plays.

The first reason for not investing is due to a simple fact. The market and technology have changed. Many years ago, the market was capitalized in manufacturing, steel, cars, etc. It was a safe bet to buy GM shares for the grandkids. It is hard to put GM out of business. It takes much money and

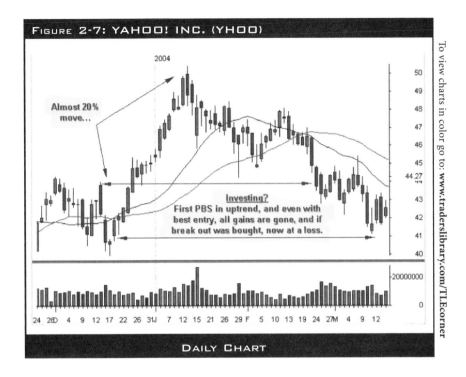

Figure 2-7: Yahoo! Inc. (YHOO)

Almost 20% move...

2004

Investing?
First PBS in uptrend, and even with best entry, all gains are gone, and if break out was bought, now at a loss.

DAILY CHART

time and resources like big factories, etc. What about today? The capitalization is in services and high technology. Is there a difference? Yes. As we've said, today, two kids in a garage can bring a company to its knees.

Second, the world has become increasingly unpredictable with the continued threat of terrorism, wars around the globe, and a nuclear threat. These things can turn the market quickly and for long periods. We have recently seen the affect of this. Volatile markets are here to stay.

Third, it was cost prohibitive to trade years ago. Commissions were as high as $500.00, and some actually higher. The spreads (difference between the bid and ask, or the amount you would pay if you bought and sold at market) were usually 3/8ths or in today's numbers, 37 cents, and as high as several dollars on high priced thin stocks. And how did you buy a stock on the move? If you had to call your broker (the only option back then), you would not participate on a quick move up; you would end up buying at the end. For that matter, how would you even know there was a quick move up? Intraday charts have only been around a relatively short time.

Today, commissions are almost free, $7.00-19.00 compared to $500.00. The 'spreads' are now down to a penny in many cases. Real-time executions with direct access platforms mean that you can buy a stock the exact second you want it, in most cases. No calls to the broker. Compare the difference. If you wanted to day trade 1,000 shares of INTC years ago, and you made a mistake and wanted to get out immediately, that mistake would have cost you $1,375.00 or so. Two commissions and 1,000 shares multiplied by a spread of 37.5 cents. That is quite a 'mistake. Today it may cost you only $35.00. That would come from two commissions at $12.50 and 1,000 shares at a one-cent spread. Looking at it another way, years ago, that 1,000 shares of INTC would have to move 1.37 cents just to break even! Day-trading, even swing trading, was not an option.

We have options today that were not available. Becoming a self-directed trader can be very satisfying even if your only goal is to mange your IRA better. The alternative is you can continue to trust your 'broker'.

Reversal Times

Anytime I am talking to a group of people that are not Pristine traders, I will ask how many of them are familiar with intraday reversal times. I estimate less than 10% of the people raise their hand on average, and those that do are only familiar because they remember reading about them in *Tools and Tactics for the Master Day Trader*. When I tell the group that I consider trading intraday without being intimately familiar with reversal times a 'huge disadvantage', most people get interested.

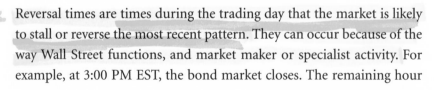

Reversal times are times during the trading day that the market is likely to stall or reverse the most recent pattern. They can occur because of the way Wall Street functions, and market maker or specialist activity. For example, at 3:00 PM EST, the bond market closes. The remaining hour of the stock market may take a direction based on the finality of having bonds closed.

Another example is during the first five minutes of the trading day, from 9:30-9:35 AM, EST. During this time the public's orders to buy and sell 'at market' are being handled by market makers and specialists. It is not unusual to see big swings in a stock's price during the first 5 minutes. A high or low may be set in the stock's price that lasts for most or even all of the trading day.

Yet another example is the beginning and ending of lunch. The reason is as simple as the fact that the market makers and specialists go to lunch, leaving junior people in charge to watch things while they are gone. Not only does this lead to reversal times going into and out of lunch, but also a phenomenon known as the 'doldrums', where you will find on most days, breakouts and breakdowns will fail during the lunch doldrums.

The list of times that should be watched are as follows, all Eastern Standard Time (EST): 9:35, 9:50-10:10, 10:25-10:35, 11:15, 12:00, 1:30, 2:15, 3:00, 3:30. Of these, the major ones to watch are 9:50-10:10, 11:15, 1:30, 2:15 and 3:00. See figure 2-8 for an example of a 5-minute chart of KLAC.

Notice the areas identified on the chart. The 9:35 reversal time (RT) sets the low of the day. The Pristine Sell Set-up (see Appendix A) that occurs at 10:00 sets a high of the day that lasts until 2:15. It is not uncommon for traders to purchase during the first 5 minutes and sell into the 10:00 RT. Notice that the 'lunchtime doldrums' delivers a 'false' breakdown, which is expected. That leads to a slow rally that challenges the high of the day. The pullback from that rally, now out of the doldrums, sets up a Pristine Buy Set-up at 2:15 RT. This leads to a powerful break out, and a new high of the day. Naturally, that rally ends at 3:00 RT, which marks the high of the day. The high of the day, the low of the day, the two next biggest pivots, and the best buy set up all happened at reversal times.

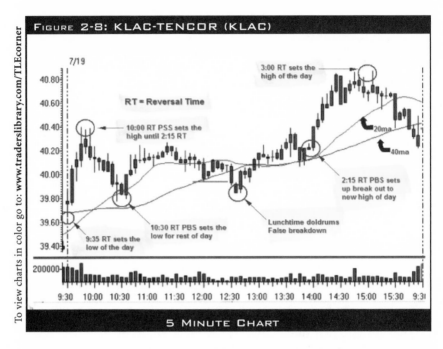

I did not look long or hard to find this chart. Check it out for yourself. Pull up your favorite charts or the market itself and notice the times listed above. It is not that every reversal time will have a major market move, but notice the major pivots, highs and lows in a stock's price every day and you will be amazed how often these major moves happen at or within one five-minute bar of a reversal time. Just notice how often a 10:30 reversal time has set the high or low of the day in the recent market. The importance of the various times may change some in different market environments, but if you time your strategies with key reversal times, they will be all the more effective.

The All Important 200 Period Moving Average

Trading is a world of probabilities. There are few things that traders can count on to happen for sure. We accept that and follow rules that keep us where the probabilities lie in our favor.

If there was one thing that I had to pick as an example of a rule that follows those probabilities more than ever, it would be the 200 period moving average and its power to stop the strongest of rallies, support a fast falling stock, and propel stocks to new highs or lows once crossed, if you know what to look for.

To appreciate how common these occurrences are, you must appreciate the research that went into finding the accompanying graphs... NONE. Often, in writing a book like this, the author may look hard trying to find the perfect example. These stocks were picked from a play log over the last week, and three weeks back for the MSFT chart, because it was a play that stuck out in my mind.

For the intraday trader, the staples we live by are the 20 and 200 period moving averages on the 5- and 15-minute chart. These are the 'Big 4'. The king of these is the 200 on the 15- minute chart. At Pristine, we have given it the pet name of "Hoss" (from "Bonanza" fame, for those of you who are over 40 or watch PAX TV).

Take a look at the 15-minute chart of IWOV (Figure 2-9), which covers a 2-day trading period.

Note that on these days, this stock could have been played long by either one of two strategies. First, the pullback to support a reversal time, 10:00 (EDT), or the 30 minute high. Either way, if you were looking for a target to sell all or half of your shares, it was not hard to find. Rule 1: If you are long on a stock that is rallying a distance into the 200 MA on the 15-minute chart, exit some or all of your shares (depending on your strategy and time frame) at the 200 MA. Notice also that this chart brings out an important concept. Any moving average of importance must be thought of as an area of support or resistance, not an exact number. It is like a rubber band, not a glass plate. The fact that this moving average was "punctured" is not as important as realizing that this general area will be one the stock must deal with. Only upon a successful retest and a move higher after the stall, should you consider the moving average to have yielded.

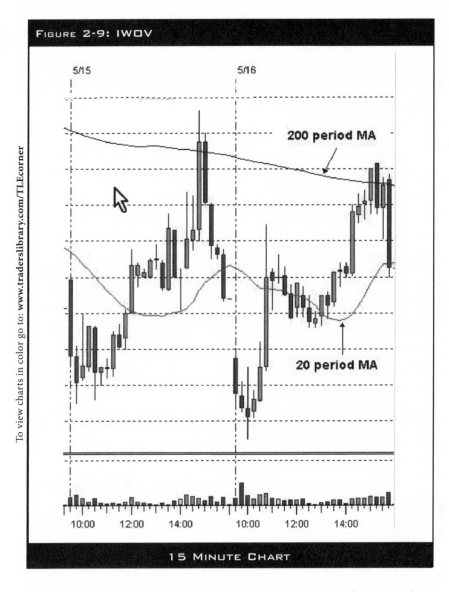

FIGURE 2-9: IWOV

200 period MA

20 period MA

5/15   5/16

10:00   12:00   14:00   10:00   12:00   14:00

15 MINUTE CHART

To view charts in color go to: www.traderslibrary.com/TLEcorner

All of the charting techniques we use work on all time frames and on all stocks, indices, futures, etc. Take a look at the Semiconductor Sector Index over the last two weeks (Figure 2-10).

Notice that on May 10 the index took out the prior day's high during the first 15 minutes of trading. A sign of power. The astute trader would realize, however, that the combination of a powerful run, right into the 200 MA on the 15-minute chart, occurring at reversal time (9:50 - 10:00), was destined to be halted even though it was free and clear of the prior day's high. While the halt of a rally is common, what happens then depends on many things. In this case, the stock takes four days to recover.

Notice on May 15, this index makes a late day breakout and rallies hard for one hour. This is the first time that this index has traded over its 30-minute high since it encountered the "200-15" three days earlier. Again, stopped cold by our friend. Since astute traders know that the NASDAQ index rarely goes very far without the Semis, those traders involved in NASDAQ stocks were taking profits on the longs both times the Semis hit the 200-15.

So, never play a stock to break over the 200-15? No, that is not the rule. Any good swing trade will usually involve crossing 'Hoss'. It just may take some time to do it. Intraday traders will usually be out of a stock when it hits 'Hoss'. There are times when stocks can be watched to see it they

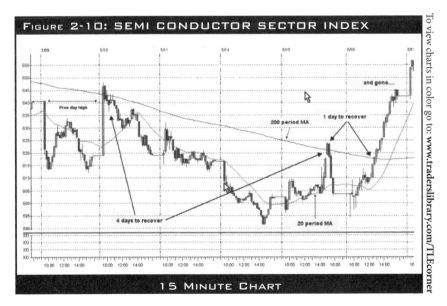

FIGURE 2-10: SEMI CONDUCTOR SECTOR INDEX

Prev day high

200 period MA

4 days to recover

20 period MA

1 day to recover

and gone.....

15 MINUTE CHART

To view charts in color go to: www.traderslibrary.com/TLEcorner

break through this mighty average. Notice on the Semi Conductor chart, after attacking and failing to break through on May 15, the index pulls back to a support level, the base from which it broke out two hours prior. This base holds and the next day the index is knocking on the door again. It took four days the first time, now only about four hours this time. The index is stronger and now the third time is the charm. Notice what happens when it does break through. There is no doubt about it, and it puts on an incredible rally. You will find this to be true quite often. This is an example of attacking the 200-15 three times with a shorter time, before attacking every time.

Let's go back and look at the first chart of IWOV with a few more days added (Figure 2-11). Are you curious about what happened to this stock after failing to break "Hoss" after two attempts?

The next day, on May 17, IWOV makes a small gap up just below "Hoss" and immediately trades straight through. Again, the third time is the charm. More important, though, is the fact that after the second failure, IWOV does not pull back far. The gap up and blast right through "Hoss" (the 200 MA on the 15-minute chart) are powerful signs of the change, and the stock continues straight up for a day and a half.

There is another way to play the break of the 200 period moving average, by 'basing'. Let's look at a couple of examples and some different time frames.

Next is a chart of Microsoft (Figure 2-12 page 66).

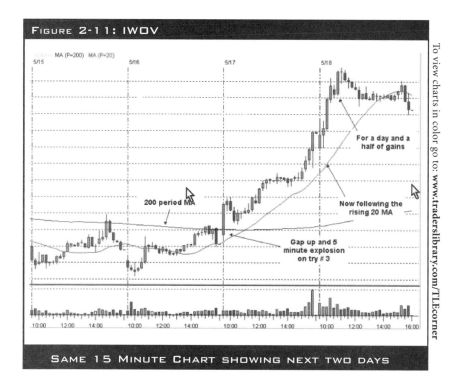

FIGURE 2-11: IWOV

SAME 15 MINUTE CHART SHOWING NEXT TWO DAYS

On May 4, MSFT set up a base just under the 200 period moving average on the 5-minute chart (yes, 'Little Joe', if you must know). Notice the picture perfect set-up as the lows keep getting higher from 10:15 until 11:45 finding support from the rising 20 period moving average on this 5-minute chart. Every line on this chart is .20, so MSFT moved from about 69.60 on the breakout to over 71 at close.

Basing under any moving average is a powerful way to overcome it. The base must be long, very close to the moving average, and tight. If not tight, then getting tighter with a series of higher lows. When this happens, the break above the moving average is usually a very powerful thing. What was once bad is now good. Yes, all of the above is true, in reverse, for shorts. No, we don't have any nicknames for the 20 period moving averages on the 5-and 15-minute charts.

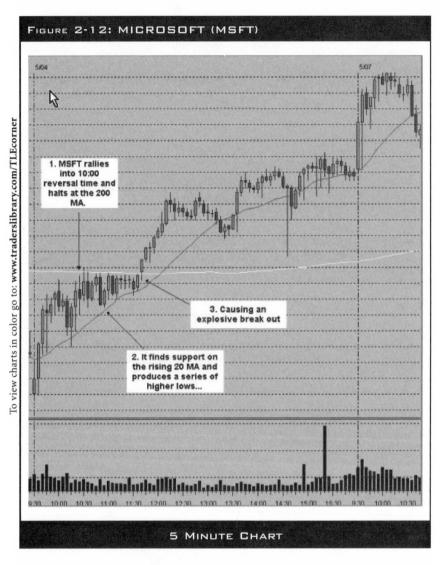

FIGURE 2-12: MICROSOFT (MSFT)

1. MSFT rallies into 10:00 reversal time and halts at the 200 MA.

3. Causing an explosive break out

2. It finds support on the rising 20 MA and produces a series of higher lows...

5 MINUTE CHART

We would be incomplete talking about the 200 period moving average if we did not include a daily chart with a 200 moving average. Let's take a look at one more example (Figure 2-13).

We only need to look back a couple days to May 17 and to the stock, the all-important General Electric (GE). This stock had been basing for 13 days just under the 200 period moving average on the daily chart. The

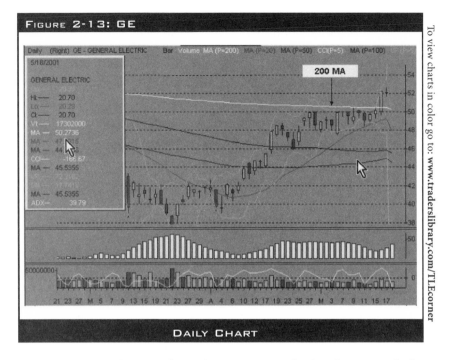

FIGURE 2-13: GE

DAILY CHART

base was also at the round number, 50. Once the break occurred, the stock was under way. These breaks often take stocks on short term rallies, moving to new areas of the chart.

In summary, the 200 period moving average should be on all of your charts. It serves the same function on all time frames. A rally stopper, a big supporter, and often a new trend setter. I hope these examples help show why sometimes resistance is resistance and, at other times, it is the beginning of a new leg up.

Moving Averages, the Power of the 20 M.A.

In a previous lesson, I discussed the tremendous power of the 200 period moving average in all time frames. I would now like to follow up and discuss the use of intraday time frames and moving averages.

The intraday trader lives off of the 5- and 15-minute charts. The main moving averages on both of these charts are the 20 and 200. We use simple moving averages, based on the close. These four moving averages (the 20 on the 5 and 15, and the 200 on the 5 and 15) make a powerful team that can be used for intraday trading. While you may want a couple more on your daily charts, this is all that is needed on the intraday charts. The 60-minute uses the same moving averages, the 20 and 200.

Many may ask why this line on the chart matters? Why do stocks respond to them? Is it just because everyone is looking at them? Yes, that can be one of the answers. A 200 period moving average is looked at by most all traders and investors. It is often considered the dividing line between an 'uptrend' and a 'downtrend'. So, when a stock pulls back to the 200 period moving average, and all can see it has held the stock before, many will buy there. This 'self fulfilling prophecy' idea is one of the reasons.

The second reason is the fact that, by the nature of how they are calculated, moving averages can act as a 'timing mechanism'. For example, a stock gaps up at open. It slowly pulls back. Strong stocks will pull back slowly and eventually find support. Very strong stocks will base sideways and 'correct through time'. The question is, when have they 'corrected' and when is it time to move on? Often, the faster moving average, the 20, has the answer.

For an example, take a look at figure 2-14. Both of the charts presented here are the same stock, same day. It is OPWV for November 13. The first is a 5-minute chart.

OPWV gapped up on this day. You can see that in the chart, as the open price on the 13th is well above the closing price of the prior day. So this stock was strong at open. Do you buy it at open? No. We would not buy stock at the open that gaps up excessively. How far will it pull back? That is where the rising 20 period moving average can be handy. In the morning, strong stocks that pull back will often find support on the rising 20 period moving average on the 5 minute chart. Notice, that at 11:30, it takes the stock to new highs.

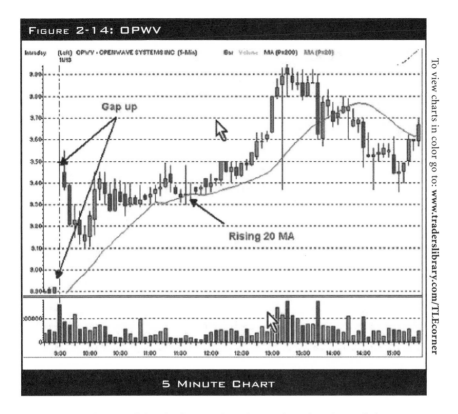

Figure 2-14: OPWV

5 Minute Chart

Stock will often pull back during lunch or shortly after, if they were strong during lunch. How far do they pull back? We will turn again to our friend, the 20 period moving average, except on a 15-minute chart this time (Figure 2-15).

Notice this is the same stock, same day. Look again at the first chart, the 5-minute. We can see at 3:10 that the stock found support, but how would you know? Well, look at the chart above. You can see that it was the 20 on the 15 that was the support. In the afternoon, strong stocks that pull back will often find support on the rising 20 period moving average on the 15-minute chart. Note that this pushed the stock to new highs and continues into the next day.

A few points to make. First, it is not hard to find these examples. I looked at my plays from yesterday and the second one I checked was OPWV.

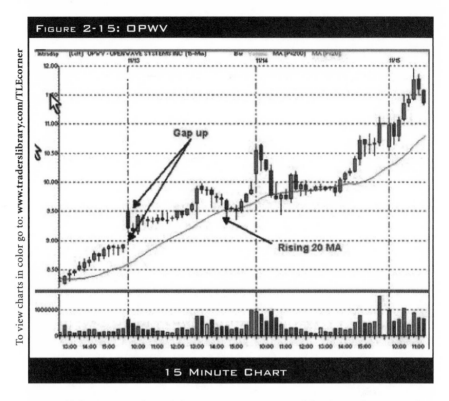

FIGURE 2-15: OPWV

15 MINUTE CHART

You will find examples of these, many times and both in the same day, like here.

Second, notice on the 15-minute chart that at 3:10 the price did go below the moving average, forming a 'tail'. This is natural. Remember, moving averages are not like pieces of glass that will break if touched. They are more like rubber bands. They are areas to be watched. A moving average is not the 'entry'. It tells you to watch for the entry.

Third, notice how multiple time frames come into play. For even better direction on longer term plays like day trades or even swings, look for the same moving averages on the 60- minute, or hourly, chart.

I hope this has provided you with some insight on how intraday charts and moving averages can help your trading.

A Return to Some Basics

It is a common and true cliché in many fields. Look at successful football dynasties. The ones that last beyond a one-season wonder always have one thing in common. They became successful by returning to basics. Nothing could be truer in the world of trading.

In trading, it is often the basics that elude many traders. They get so wrapped up in so many fancy indicators and techniques that they ignore the necessary elements that they first learned by being so critical. This is especially true in the current market. Knowing both the macro and micro stages of the current market, and what strategies and targets would be applicable for that market, should be a part of every trader's daily routine.

Many get so involved looking for specific patterns in only one time frame that they do not even consider that the pattern may be best left alone this week. Many do not even know or understand the concept of looking at multiple time frames. This concept requires that to get the odds in your favor, you want to have both the 'macro' time frame and the 'micro' time frame pointing in the same direction.

Having a plan of what you want to do every day is critical. Assessing your money management and deciding how much should be risked in uncertain environments in both long and short-term accounts is crucial to successful trading.

How do you try to increase your odds in taking plays? Look for the best entries on plays that focus on the current environment. Below is an example of a trade from the stock 'MRK', which was posted as a buy at 53.10 January 28, 2003. It was sold on the gap up on January 30, 2003 at 55.75 (Figure 2-16).

The strategy discussion is as follows. MRK was looking like a possible Climactic Buy Set-up (looks for stocks on daily charts that have recently experienced climactic declines on big volume, which renders them oversold and overdue for a sharp rebound) on January 28. It was hitting a prior support area from November 13, 2002. It was extended to the downside. The only problem is that the volume was not really 'climactic' as we define it. Note that the Climactic Buy Set-up is used sparingly, as it is one of the few strategies I teach that 'fights the trend'. There are exact requirements for entry. (Don't try this at home, kids!) Also, the market was bearish at this time, not looking favorably on long plays in general, and our plan was not to be in a swing long at this time.

So what was the answer? On the morning of the 28th, MRK gapped up for us. This gap filled the requirements of another strategy, a guerilla tactic known as a "Bullish Gap Surprise." So while we had a questionable long trade, we had an entry provided by a separate, overlapping strategy. The entry, and target, were 'by the book' per the guerilla tactic.

Follow a plan, know what stage of the market you are in, and manage your trades and money accordingly. Track and analyze what you do, and remember to always return to the basics.

FIGURE 2-16: MEREK & CO TRADE (MRK)

Chapter 3
Lessons on Managing

Managing a Trade

The title of this lesson really encompasses many topics. I want to focus on the criteria here that determine your profit-to-loss ratio and share size. While this is not the first step in picking a trade, it is the most important.

Let's look at the whole process. You are scanning charts for trades. You should be looking for pictures of your favorite strategies. Once you find a picture that matches a strategy in your trading plan, you want to ensure that elements such as futures timing and relative strength are in place before you make the trade. All these topics are important and worthy of discussion. For now, I want to focus first on determining if the trade is worthy based on the trades expectancy (the potential gain versus the potential loss) and how to determine share size.

Once you have a trade in mind, the chart can help you determine where the logical stop loss point and the potential target would be. These things come from the chart and are fixed. They cannot be moved about randomly. They are dictated by the rules of your strategy. Therefore, you want to make sure that the ratio of potential profit to potential loss is favorable. It may vary with the strategy, but you want at least a one-to-one ratio or, preferably, a two-to-one. Sometimes, you can find much greater ratios.

Strategies for Profiting on Every Trade

Let's take an example. You find a Pristine Buy Set-up (see Appendix A) on a daily chart. You like the picture. Following the rules of the strategy, you would seek to buy over yesterday's high. Let's see what the expectancy would be. The stop would be under yesterday's low. Lets say yesterday's bar was not very narrow. The resulting stop may be $2.00. If the stock was not in a Stage 2 uptrend, your target may be limited to a 40 percent retracement from the recent high to the current pull back area. Let's say that number ends up being $1.50. You would be risking $2.00 to make $1.50 (expectancy 1.5/2 = .75). This is not a good idea unless you had a history of being almost 100 percent successful with this trade.

This is why narrow range days are good on Pristine Buy Set-ups and why Stage 2 uptrends also are good. In a better set up, you may find a target of $3.00, and if the prior day had a range of only $1.00, the stop would be only $1.00. This would be a $1.00 risk for a possible $3.00 reward, based on the chart and the strategy for the stop and target. That is a three-to-one expectancy and a much better ratio.

If you do not like the trade, you may pass. You may *not* change the target or stop at random just to make the expectancy number work. Many new traders make that mistake. The expectancy is built into the chart.

What is a good expectancy? It may vary depending on your style of trading. It will also vary with the chance of success on a particular play. For example a micro scalper (someone who trades large shares for 10 cent profits) may go with a one-to-one expectancy because he is right 80 percent of the time. Many longer-term traders are successful only 40 percent of the time because the expectancy is three or more to one on long term plays. For example, they go for $12.00 while risking $3.00, for example.

Once you know the expectancy is good, you may decide to enter the trade. In that case, you must decide on the number of shares. Many people play a fixed number of shares. Many vary the size with the price of the stock. These are not good formulas if you want to maximize the chances of making money in the long term. I suggest you decide on the number of shares by keeping the risk the same on each trade. To do this, you need to know your stop loss and the maximum amount of loss you are willing to take on a trade. This maximum loss number derives from your Trading Plan. Simply play the number of shares that allow a stop to hit your fixed, predetermined maximum loss amount. If you want to keep any one loss to $300, and the stop loss on this trade is 50 cents, then you need to play 600 shares. A 50-cent loss on 600 shares would be $300. This brings every trade to an equal footing no trades are riskier except for the stock volatility and the difficulty of getting out at the stop number.

These ideas should be part of every decision to enter a trade. Note that under this method, you cannot even enter a trade until you determine the stop, because you would not even know how many shares to play. Now, once you've entered the trade, then you must decide how long to hold it.

Dealing with Disaster

Holding trades overnight has certain benefits and risks. I consider it necessary for a trading plan to have a Wealth Building Account for swing and core trades, which would all be overnight holds. So, following your trading plan and playing the proper share size are very important. If you are careful, over time the benefits should outweigh the risks. However, no matter how careful you are, you will have a morning where a position you have is gapping open against you.

Remember, there are no stops overnight. Let us say you are long on XYZ at $30.00 and, at 7:00 AM EST the next morning, company XYZ makes some announcements. Let us say they are going to miss their next earnings number, the CEO just resigned, and they suspect they have accounting problems.

There is a good chance (about 99.99 percent) that when trading starts the next morning at 8:00 A.M. EST (pre-market trading starts with ECNs at this time) that your stock will be trading much lower. Let's say at 8:00 it starts trading at $26.00. From 8:00-9:30 it ranges from $26.00 – $25.00.

Then at 9:00 it opens at 25.10. It will not matter that you have a stop in place at $28.50. During pre-market, stops are not in effect. Then, when the market opens, your stop will be filled (if it is GTC-good till cancelled-or if you re-entered it at open) at the best price at the time—$25.10—not your desired price of $28.50.

So, how do you handle these disaster situations? Here are some tips to better manage these situations in the best way over the long term.

First, do not panic. Easy to say, but hard to do unless you have a strategy in place.

Second, ignore the pre-market trading. From 8:00 until 9:30, only ECNs are trading; some stocks don't trade at all. If your stock is gapping down like this, it will likely be trading, but trading erratically.

Third, when the market opens officially at 9:30 EST, do nothing for five minutes. That's right, just watch it. After five minutes, mark off the low and put a stop for half your shares—$.05-.10 under that 5-minute low.

Fourth, let it trade for 30 minutes. Then put a stop for the other half of your shares–$.05-.10 under that 30-minute low. At this point, if the stock did not violate the 5-minute low, you will still have all your shares, half with a stop under the 5-minute low, half under the 30-minute low.

You will often find you still have all of your shares, or at least half. Often, after a large gap, the opening half hour puts in the lows for the upcoming days. If your shares do stop, usually you are risking a relatively small amount extra.

From there, you can treat the trade as a swing with a one-day trailing stop, or the stock may rebound to prior levels and you can follow your prior plan. While the example given was for a gap down on a long position, the same rules hold true for gapping up on a short position. Use 5- and 30-minute highs as stops.

Such a disaster plan will help you minimize the losses over the long term.

Alternate Swing Entries

Swing trading refers to taking trades that traders intend to hold for two to five days. Their intent is to capture the meat or a move in a short period of time. It is not unusual to capture in a few days the same percentage gain that the stock might make all year long. Stocks frequently rally, and then give back all their gains, leaving the longe-term investor with nothing to show for the move, or even a loss.

We typically look to the daily chart to find patterns that would allow for low risk entries. Sometimes, we can use an hourly chart. We tend to seek stocks that are in strong trends, staying in or breaking out of bases (consolidations) or occasionally extremely over bought/oversold.

Once we find a favorable pattern, the usual entry involves buying the stock over the prior day's high, or shorting under the prior day's low. This is because the prior day's high or low involves a resistance or support area, and breaking this area is a sign of strength or weakness that a trader wants to see before taking a trade. It is the line in the sand that must be crossed. This entry criterion often will keep you out of trades that never perform and will increase the success rate of those trades that are entered.

For someone who is trading part time, this may be the only option. If a trader works another job full time or is occupied during trading hours trades can be entered by placing buy and sell stop orders with a broker, and calling to adjust the buy and sell stops once the trade is entered. However, if you sit with the market all day, there are other entries that you can use. Some are necessary alternatives that come into play when the stock gaps. Some are used to enhance the possible reward-to-risk ratio

First is the situation that happens when a stock gaps up excessively. Because a large gap up may bring in selling, purchasing the stock immediately just because it is over the entry price (yesterday's high of the day) may be unwise. You may be buying the high of the day. There may be a better entry later. I consider any gap of 50 cents or more (on average priced stocks) above the proposed entry (or prior day's high, whichever is higher) as excessive and the entry invalid. However, you may still have a play. As long as the stock does not rally hard for the first 30 minutes, you can use the 30-minute high as an alternate entry. Let the stock trade for 30 minutes, and mark off the high. That is your new entry.

Those with more experience intraday may look at another option. Stocks that gap up often pullback and sell off for 20-60 minutes. They sometimes come back to the prior day's closing price. We call this "filling the gap." Buying the stock on a 5-minute Pristine Buy Set-up (see Appendix A) after the gap fill can be a low-risk way to play the stock long.

Sometimes a guerrilla tactic may provide an entry to a swing trade. Guerrilla tactics are very specific tactics that are often based on just a one- or two- bar set-up. They sometimes involve gaps (when a stock opens at a higher or lower price than it closed at the prior day). See figure 3-1 for example.

MNST gapped down on the last bar on the daily chart. This play on MNST will show us three ways to play this chart other than waiting for the low of the prior day, which is a wide bar. First, this gap was actually a bearish gap surprise; the entry is either an immediate entry or a 5-minute low, which would have you in very early. While the holding time for the guerrilla tactic is shorter, the trade eventually does trade under the prior day's low and a swing portion of the position could then be held. This entry would be the earliest of them all.

If you did not play that entry, there is another alternative. Sometimes, the prior day's high is so far away that waiting for this entry will cause the stop to be so wide that the reward-to-risk ratio becomes too low to take the trade. If the stock is otherwise in the area we want to play, we will look at a 30-minute entry as being an alternative, even if the stock does not gap up. This is because it takes a good measure of strength to trade over the high of the day after 30 minutes. While this entry is not as reli-

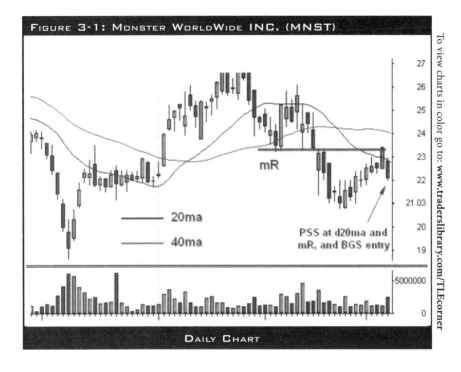

able as the prior day's high, when you consider the increased reward-to risk aspects, it is an excellent alternative.

Sometimes intraday analysis and patterns can give you a similar entry, other than the 30-minute high. For example, if a bullish base sets up, but is under the high of the day, you can use it as a substitute entry. At this point, the swing entry is almost anticipatory, and you will want to see the real entry hit to stay with the position as a swing. Your reward-to-risk can be greatly enhanced on these plays, which will make up for the fact that the entries are not as reliable.

As an example, look at the hourly chart that formed on MNST, below (Figure 3-2). This shows the day after the last in the daily chart shown above. Here, we are waiting until after the play dropped a bit (or, if you may not have seen this chart until the bearish entry bar formed). So how do we get in the next day? This stock looks lower because this is a powerful pattern. Using the current stop provided by the wide bar, the reward–to-risk would be hard to justify. So we can look intraday.

Here, four higher lows formed on the hourly chart into the declining 20-period moving average (d20ma), as the stock retraced some of the drop it had the day before. You can short the hourly Pristine Sell Set-up that formed where the arrow is. This gives a much tighter stop because the stop is placed over the high of that small red bar (arrow). The target then reverts to the daily chart.

In summary, you need to choose an entry and management style that fits your personality and schedule. You should also monitor what you do carefully. It is not uncommon for intraday traders to over manage perfectly good swing positions that are better left alone. Understand also that whenever you alter the stop from the daily chart to increase the risk reward, there is a trade-off. The play is more likely to stop, which decreases its overall success rate.

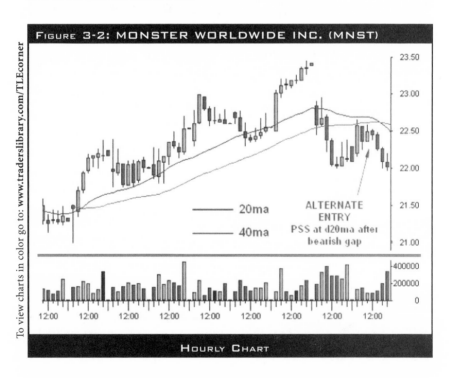

FIGURE 3-2: MONSTER WORLDWIDE INC. (MNST)

20ma
40ma

ALTERNATE ENTRY
PSS at d20ma after bearish gap

HOURLY CHART

The Reward to Risk Ratio

You have found a trade that meets the criteria that the strategy requires. What determines if you take the trade? What if there are dozens of these trades that you can find every hour that meet the criteria, but you are able to trade only four, or two, or one? How do you determine the best one?

One of the things you will do is try to find the best examples of quality in the trade you take. Naturally, all trades that meet your minimum criteria are not the same. The reward-to-risk ratio is another thing you can look at to determine if you take any particular trade. The reward-to-risk ratio, or "RR" is the amount to be made from the entry to the target, compared to the amount to be lost from the entry to the stop.

Many traders will demand that the possible RR for a trade be a certain number, like three-to-one (going for a three dollar target with a one dollar stop), or maybe even much higher. Certainly you would not risk a dollar to make a dollar.

There is a tradeoff in the RR you pick. Very simply, though the high RR trades sound, and often are, the best, they have the lowest odds of being obtained. So while going for three-to-one sounds better than one-to-one, if you get only the three-to-one trade right one in four times, you are losing money. If you get the one-to-one trade right two out of three times, you are making money. Naturally, the one-to-one trade will be easier to achieve. So you need to analyze every trade based on the RR presented, and the likelihood that you will achieve that RR consistently. You can determine your odds by tracking your results on a trade over a period of time to see how successful you are.

Let's take a look at a sample trade. Below are the daily charts of CRDN and the intraday 5-minute chart for the last day on the daily chart (Figure 3-3). On the last day on the chart, CRDN gapped up.

The play is set up properly, and would call for an entry either immediately or over the 5-minute high, with a stop under yesterday's low. This is the recommended entry and stop. The recommended management sets up certain odds for the play, and may be desirable because it is the best way to manage this trade, or perhaps it is best if it is going to be entered or managed while at work. Sometimes intraday traders find alternate methods of entering and managing the trade.

Whenever you stray from recommended strategies, the odds start changing. However, if managed properly, the outcome can be more profitable. Lets examine the odds of changing the stop from yesterday's low, to today's low (today's low is 33.95). We will use the 5-minute high for entry. Study the tables in figures 3-4 and 3-5.

In all of these scenarios, we will keep the target the same. The goal here is to compare entries and RR options. Notice that for every successful trade, the option using today's LOD (low of day) stop makes almost twice as much money. This is based on share sizing so that all trades have the same risked dollars. (If you use a constant share size, then the loss would be almost half, so the same concept applies.) What this is saying is that though the odds of this trade stopping out are more likely using the tighter stop, it could stop out almost twice as much and still yield the

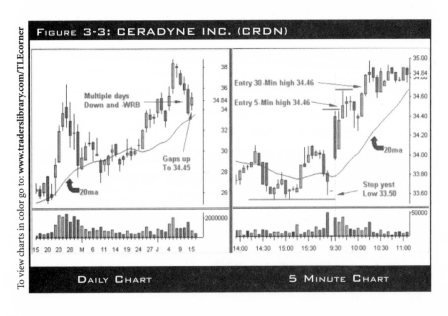

82

same amount of money. So determine if your trades hold the stop at least half as much using the tight stop. If yes, then it is the better option.

Let's look at changing the entry criteria (Figure 3-6). A trader may say that waiting for the 30-minute high will make the trade at higher odds of success. While this may be true, the RR could change so much at the 30-minute high that it may not make sense.

FIGURE 3-4: SCENARIO 1, BY THE BOOK, YEST LOD STOP

5 minute high	$34.46
Stop under yesterday's low	$33.50
Target same for all...36.00	$36.00
Risk	$0.96
Reward	$1.54
Risk $$ Sample	$500.00
Profit if target	$802.08

FIGURE 3-5: SCENARIO 2, BY THE BOOK, TODAY LOD STOP

5 minute high	$34.46
Stop under yesterday's low	$33.95
Target same for all...36.00	$36.00
Risk	$0.51
Reward	$1.54
Risk $$ Sample	$500.00
Share Size	980
Loss if stopped	$500.00
Profit if target	$1,509.80

In this case, the 30-minute high is not that far away, so the profit does not change much. It is lower, and the question is, will this entry produce enough success to make up for the lower dollars made every time?

Now let's take a look at entering by combining this with another tactic (Figure 3-7). Lets buy the Pristine Buy Set-up (see Appendix A) on the pullback to support at reversal time.

CRDN pulled back to support during the very first reversal time, 9:35 EST. This requires a 1-minute chart to be used. The entry is over the high of that lowest 1-minute bar, and a stop could revert back to yesterday's low, or for the true 1-minute PBS, under the low of the same bar. This reduces the risk tremendously. Let's look at the scenarios of using these options (Figures 3-8 and 3-9 page 86).

Using the prior day's low reduces this profit about the same as using the 5-minute high with today's LOD stop. This is just a coincidence. Taking the 1-minute PBS with that earlier entry keeps the RR the same even though you are now using yesterday's stop. The drawback is that using

FIGURE 3-6: SCENARIO 3, 30 MINUTE HIGH, YEST LOD STOP	
30 minute high	$34.66
Stop under yesterday's low	$33.50
Target same for all...36.00	$36.00
Risk	$1.16
Reward	$1.34
Risk $$ Sample	$500.00
Share Size	431
Loss if stopped	$500.00
Profit if target	$577.59

this entry is no guarantee that the stock will continue to move up. Many more will stop out.

Last is the ultimate in RR—using the 1-minute entry and stop. This now creates 4 to 12 times the profit when the target is hit. The analysis must now be made: can the target be achieved often enough under these tight entries and stop criteria to produce more dollars on a regular basis? Again, tracking your plays under different options will help you to complete this analysis for any tactic you choose to study.

FIGURE 3-7: CERADYNE INC. (CRDN)

Pullback to gap fill @ 9:35 reversal time

20ma

1-Min PBS Entry 34.08 Stop 33.95

15:40 15:45 15:50 15:55 9:30 9:35 9:40 9:45 9:50

1 MINUTE CHART

To view charts in color go to: www.traderslibrary.com/TLEcorner

FIGURE 3-8: SCENARIO 4, PBS ON PULLBACK, YEST LOD STOP	
PBS entry	$34.08
Stop under yesterday's low	$33.50
Target same for all...36.00	$36.00
Risk	$0.58
Reward	$1.92
Risk $$ Sample	$500.00
Share Size	862
Loss if stopped	$500.00
Profit if target	$1,655.17

FIGURE 3-9: SCENARIO 5, PBS ON PULLBACK, 1 MIN PBS STOP	
PBS entry	$34.08
Stop under yesterday's low	$33.95
Target same for all...36.00	$36.00
Risk	$0.13
Reward	$1.92
Risk $$ Sample	$500.00
Share Size	3846
Loss if stopped	$500.00
Profit if target	$7,384.62

Do You Find Yourself Target Challenged?

One of the greatest challenges in trading comes from getting to targets. It is one of the most difficult areas both from a technical perspective (finding the right areas on the charts) to a psychological perspective (staying with the trade while the stock achieves that target).

Psychologically, this is perhaps the most difficult area because you may not even know you have the problem. If you don't take stops, you see and feel the pain immediately. You may fix it, or may not, but you know what you have to deal with and you cannot avoid it. If you do a poor job reaching targets, you may not notice the problem. You may even feel you are doing well because you feel like you have a lot of winners. The only problem is that you have a handful of losers that wipe out all the small gains. Without tracking and evaluating the statistics on your trades, you may never realize the importance of this issue. This is where most people stand. Let's take a look at which issues to consider when setting targets.

Unless you are breaking to new highs, you will *always* encounter some levels of resistance. The question is, at which point will the supply overcome the demand? You need to examine the quality of the trend and the quality of the current breakout. Next, you have to look at the quality of the resistance you are encountering.

First, consider the quality of the trend—or the price pattern being played. Different price patterns leading into the play will have different power to drive the stock. Strong uptrends and downtrends are always nice here because they will go through the first areas of supply and demand. After all, an uptrend is a series of higher highs and higher lows. Long bases and wide range bars also help provide the momentum to continue prices through congested areas.

Second, the type of breakout that happens can help fuel the stock in the short term to overcome areas of supply and demand. Here, stocks that create shocking or surprising moves can fuel a stock through supply or demand areas. Examples are, stocks that gap out of long bases or professional gaps that go against the current trend.

Third, different levels of resistance have different meanings. Single pivots formed against a strong trend are the easiest to break. Long bases and failed breakouts will have the highest level of supply or demand. This is especially true when they are on the right side of the prevailing trend.

To use an analogy, imagine a car or truck driving down the road and crashing into a wall. The pattern is analogous to whether you are in a small car or a huge truck. The breakout is analogous to the speed at which you are traveling, and the target is the type of wall you are about to hit.

A mortgage gap that also gaps over a base and resumes an uptrend, that runs into a single prior pivot, is like the Mac truck going 100 miles per hour running into a wall of empty boxes. A buy set-up in a downtrend with a base above it is like an economy car coasting uphill running into a brick wall.

For an intraday chart of Apple Computer see figure 3-10. It is an example of a pattern, entry and a prior high that dictates going for more than the prior high.

Here we have a nice uptrend, a gap up, and prior high that left little supply behind. AAPL stalls at the prior high before going much higher. Selling some into the prior high and holding some for higher prices (next target is not visible on the 5-minute chart) is the key.

Next is a play from the weekly chart of Albertsons (Figure 3-11 page 90).

Here we have the momentum (big truck) of a downtrend and failed bullish bars. We have the entry triggered (speed) of a long base breaking down. Will this develop enough momentum to get beyond the first target? (see chart, "Which is target?"). To keep the analogy going, here the Mac truck, going 100 miles an hour, should get through the wall of cardboard. The real target of course is the lower one.

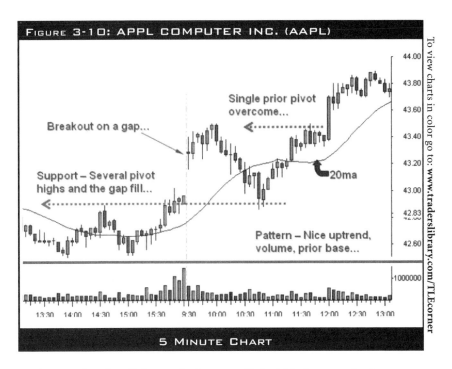

FIGURE 3-10: APPL COMPUTER INC. (AAPL)

Single prior pivot overcome...

Breakout on a gap...

Support – Several pivot highs and the gap fill...

20ma

Pattern – Nice uptrend, volume, prior base...

5 MINUTE CHART

To view charts in color go to: www.traderslibrary.com/TLEcorner

By the way, despite all the analysis, you will find hitting any single target a difficult goal. The best traders use this information to arrive at two, three or more logical exit points and sell incrementally.

To enter a trade is just as important as the exit. See the next lesson for more.

The Anatomy of an Entry

Previously I discussed the importance of exiting a trade at the right time. Getting out of a stock when you need to is the hallmark of a good trader, as is letting profits run on good trades. However, a proper entry is essential, and in many ways, the hardest part of the trade. Knowing when to play a stock or leave it alone is one issue. Here, we will talk about the exact entry into a stock once you have decided it should be in play, based on the chart pattern and the market action.

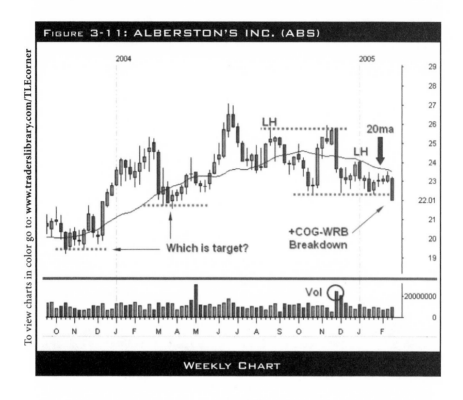

FIGURE 3-11: ALBERSTON'S INC. (ABS)

WEEKLY CHART

Once you have decided a stock should be played based on a certain strategy, you then need to enter the stock based on the strike price that the strategy dictates. However, it is not always easy. There are many rules that an astute trader should use beyond just buying above or below a certain price. We will look at many of the considerations a trader must make when looking to enter a stock properly. As an example, refer to the next chart below (Figure 3-12). This is a 5-minute chart of EFDS for May 25, 2001. The stock closed on the 24th at 24.11 and the high of the day on the 24th was 21.50. It opened on the 25th at 21.68. Assume the Pristine Buy Set-up was a good one, so we will be looking for an entry over the prior day's high. That is the correct "entry" for the "strategy" on the daily chart. Sounds easy? Let's take a look.

There are numbers on this chart representing six areas of interest. Where should this stock have been entered? Study the chart and pick an answer before proceeding.

Let's take a look. Bar #1 is the first 5-minute bar. The stock has gapped up 57 cents from the prior days close of 21.11 and over the strike price of 21.50. It is over the strike price, so do we buy here? Well first you must consider the gap. A gap of 5/8 or over (62.5 cents) would make the play invalid as this would be considered an excessive gap, and make the play unwise due to being extended. This is a good rule of thumb. Here the gap is less than 62 cents, so this rule came close but does not apply. However, an astute trader would not have bought EFDS here. Why? The spirit of the rule is to stop you from buying a stock that may be falling. This stock opened on its high and immediately traded down. An astute trader will always buy on the way up, even if it is a 30-second high that is being taken out. Since this stock never ticked up, and traded straight down for 5 minutes, an astute trader would not enter here, and would wait for a 5-minute high at this point.

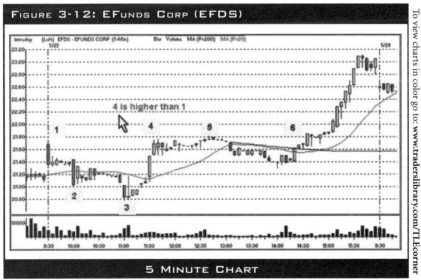

FIGURE 3-12: EFunds Corp (EFDS)

5 MINUTE CHART

To view charts in color go to: www.traderslibrary.com/TLEcorner

Bar #2 is the pullback into the 10:00 reversal time. A pullback to support at reversal is not an 'entry' for a Pristine Buy Set-up on the daily. We are looking for yesterday's high. However, even if you were looking to anticipate an early entry, pullbacks to support at reversal time are intended to take advantage of pullbacks in uptrending stocks; this stock is downtrending at 10:00. No entry available here.

Bar #3 is a new low, clearly in a downtrend on the 5-minute chart. Astute traders do not 'guess' on an entry off the bottom. This turns out to be the low of the day, but there is no entry available here off the chart.

Bar #4 is where the stock takes out the day's high. This is where most traders feel the appropriate entry lies. Since this stock 'gapped' up then pulled back, the 30-minute high can be used for a valid entry. Normally this price point would be the entry, which is the high of the day at this time of 21.68. As you may be sensing though, this is not going to be the entry for the astute trader. Why? Look how hard the stock ran to get to the day's high. It went from the low of the day to the high of the day in 30 minutes, covering almost a full point, a good move for a $21.00 stock. More time than not, this entry will be unwise. You want to attack the high from a close by base, or from a series of higher highs and higher lows that bring you close to the high to attack it from close range. Imagine the marathon runner that does the 23 miles and then you ask the runner to enter another race. He needs a rest. At this point you need to let it go and wait for a new attack on the day's high, or a pullback for proper entry.

Bar #5 occurs next, and it's the bar that takes out the newly formed high of the day. There was no pullback to speak of so the bar becomes the next possible entry. Is this valid? Once again, you must pass. Why? Lunch time doldrums. 12:45 to be exact. Most breakouts during lunch fail; as a rule, you should not be playing breakouts during lunch time.

So, we now have to wait to come out of lunch, and again look for a pullback or a new high. Bar #6 is the bar that finally takes out the high of the day at 2:40 over $2.80. Here, finally is the proper entry.

Notice that all of the other entries would have gotten you in earlier, but more times than not, the entry would have led to a stop out. Remember, missed money is better than lost money. Having the patience to wait for the proper entry is key to keeping you on the right side of the trade.

Chapter 4
Lessons on Psychology in Trading & Planning

The Psychology of Fear

You had a trade in mind all morning. You found a perfect Pristine Buy Set-up (see Appendix A) on the daily chart last night. You followed it during pre-market. It opened just below yesterday's high (your buy point) and slowly crept its way up right to that strike price. During reversal time it based sideways and did not give up an inch. Now, as the futures just start to turn up at 10:10, your stock starts to pick up in volume. The prints are going off at the offer and those offers are disappearing. When they are gone, that means it is time to buy! You watch them all disappear. Then you decide you better watch a little more 'just to make sure'. It pulls back a little, and you are thinking, "I'm glad I waited." Then it surges up and starts really moving. You try to buy at the offer, but it moved too fast. You don't chase it, and now it is gone. It turns out to be a great play. What went wrong?

Later that day you decide to buy a stock over 35.35, stop under 35, and target 35.9. You get in the stock properly at 35.39 and it moves up to 35.55. You debate if you should be taking profits now or waiting for the target. The stock starts pulling back too fast to take profits. You are now concerned as the stock has pulled back to your entry. You finally get out

94

at 35.30 for a small loss. It wasn't at the stop, but it did not feel good to be negative in the position after being up 20 cents. The stock now rallies to the target, without you. Another trade missed and a small loss taken. Does this sound like something that happens to you?

What you are experiencing are the different effects of fear. As you may be aware, psychological aspects make up 85 percent of the trading equation. Fear is one of the aspects. Ideally, we would all be "emotionless" traders; no fear, no greed, just pure discipline. While this may be a worthy goal, not many can take the leap to this level just because I say you need to. While most people cannot eliminate fear, there are some things you can do to keep it in check. That is the purpose of this lesson. Here are some suggestions:

1. First, fear's greatest enemy is a well laid plan. Have a trading plan that clearly spells out what strategies you will play, how many shares you will play, how much money you are willing to lose on a single trade. There are many aspects to this plan and they will be the topic of the next lesson.

2. Next, plan out the individual trade. When you see a trade that fits into your plan, study the play to find the proper stop loss and target. Play the proper share size so a stop out does not violate your maximum loss per trade. Make your decisions before the trade hits while you have a clear level head. Follow the plan without question. You must execute the planned trades.

3. The next step may be the most important. Let your plan go to work. Let the play finish. Unless something changes about the trade, let it come to its natural conclusion, either the target or the stop. Think about it. You have planned a trade while you had a clear head. You believe the trade is worth your hard earned money. Give it a chance to finish.

4. There are some reasons to end the trade early. Perhaps there has been a change in market environment. For example, you might be long in your play and the futures just took out key support. Or maybe you planned on reaching the target by reversal time and it is almost at the target with reversal time now here. However, these are the minority. The vast majority you should leave the play alone. Do not be jiggled out by your Level 2 screen. The chart pattern is by far more important.

5. If you are still so nervous that you can't handle it, try this next. Sell half the position at the reduced target. Get used to taking partial profits and this will let you have confidence letting the back half hit the target. This will also likely put you in a 'no lose' situation with the trade, giving you some patience. Good traders sell incrementally, on the way up, all of the time.

6. If that does not help, you need to cut back on your share size (or find a trade with a smaller stop), so the size of the potential loss does not trigger your "pain factor."

7. If these things prove helpful, you will start building the confidence needed to stay with the trades.

Remember, a well laid plan and confidence are the enemies of fear. Think of yourself as two people. First as a "planner" who develops good trades. Second, as an "executioner" whose job it is to execute the plans that have been laid out. Don't empower the "executioner" to second guess the "planner."

The Trading Plan - The Key to Your Success

There is an old cliché that says, "If you fail to plan, you will plan to fail." While this saying is true of many things in life, there is no area where it holds truer than in trading,

Previously, in this book, I have referred to a common element called a 'trading plan'. Explaining a trading plan is not that difficult. Explaining why you must have one is always a challenge, because most traders do not have one. While they all agree it is a good idea, they never seem to take the time to write one.

Do you know which strategy is your best morning strategy? Do you have exact criteria written that explains that strategy, including what the stock must look like on the daily, where it must open, and what the futures must be doing for you to take that trade? Can you right now find in writing how much is the maximum amount you are willing to lose on any one trade? Do you have a daily goal to hit financially? What do you do when you hit that goal? How much are you allowed to lose before you quit? What do you do after three winning trades? Five winning trades?

Most people just go through the day 'drifting.' Any amount of money made is never enough. Any loss does not stop the need to 'get back'. Most trades are the result of chasing someone else's idea, not following a strict strategy. If you answered yes to all of the questions above, nice going. If not, let me try to convince you.

The mind responds better to things that are written. It activates a different physical part of the brain when we write or type something. It is necessary to write. We would all like to be "emotionless traders." The closest you can come to that is to separate yourself into two people. The first should be the planner. This person writes a trading plan, puts that plan into effect by finding trades during the day, takes those trades and develops entries, stops, and targets and puts them in writing. Then a second person is the 'executioner' and has no power to change things. This person's only job is to carry out the plan. If you are able to find successful trades consistently, but you are not making money, find out why. It is likely because the executioner in you has taken over the planner. He has taken you out of trades before the target or stop, to your detriment. Or, he has ignored stops, thinking he knows better.

You should have at least four parts to your trading plan. The first part should be a very simple chart of what you would consider to be your maximum lot size on any trade for any given price of stock. You may have a maximum for $30-40 stocks, and a higher maximum for $20-30 stocks. Spell it all out. This is not necessarily your trade lot size, just a maximum you would never go over.

Next, you need to define some financial things. How much are you willing to lose on a trade? How much are you willing to lose in a day before quitting or before quitting for the morning? What is your goal per day? Per week? What do you do when you hit it? Quit? Or, do you trail stop your day's profits just like you would with a good stock? The answers you choose are not as important as having the discipline to follow them.

In this section, you should also have the calculation for your lot size per trade. You should look to risk a constant amount of money per trade. This means you need to look at the stop on a proposed trade, and calculate the share size needed to ensure a stop does not violate the maximum amount you are willing to lose on a trade.

In the third section, you will need to spell out the strategies that you will use throughout the day. If you are new, pick one or two of your favorites. Spell out the exact requirements of the stock that you will be watching and detail what your entry will be based on. What will the market have to be doing for you to take the trade? What time of day is this trade acceptable? Pass on all trades that do not fit the criteria. Try tracking your trade results by strategy for a while to see which ones truly work best for you. You may be surprised that the results may be different than what you now think.

Last, have a section for your own goals as a trader. Continuing education is important to us all. Do you want to learn options to supplement your trading? Do you want to take another seminar? Do you have a list of good books you would like to read? Need some relaxation classes?

You will find that having a trading plan and following it will improve your results almost immediately. It will keep you calmer and less stressed. It is a business plan for your trading business. Don't trade without it.

Discipline

To have a trading plan, you must be disciplined. This next lesson will expand upon the psychological topic of discipline. Unlike many of the past lessons, it will not be long. It will not have a clean-cut list of things you need to do. There will not be a simple plan that is ready to execute. There are no nicely labeled charts to tell you what to do. Discipline is a more illusive topic. Yet, if there were one lesson that you should frame and put above your computer, this would be the one.

For trading purposes, discipline can be simply defined as your ability to follow your trading plan.

Just like many past lessons, here is a reference to a trading plan. It is a simple concept. You need to define what you want to trade. You need to define when you want to trade it. You need to decide how to trade and manage it. You need to decide how to handle your account when you are making money (do you keep a trail stop on profits?). You need to handle your account when bad days come along (do you have a stop loss every day?).

Once you have this, a couple of rules are helpful. Do not change you plan during the trading day. Commit to only making changes when the market is closed. Otherwise, there is no plan at all. For at least one month, read your plan every morning before you trade. Then read every weekend. Get one of those little free applications that open programs for you at certain times of the day. Have it open your trading plan at 9:25 AM, just before you trade.

The best way to enforce discipline is just by awareness. Keep records of your trades. On every trade, include an answer to the simple question, "Was this trade part of my trading plan?" Yes or no. There is no in between. Be aware that the undisciplined traders are almost guaranteed to fail. Ask every day if you are keeping the discipline or are you just taking trades at random that look good at the moment? You can't fix something if you do not know it is broken. You must first be aware that you have a discipline problem.

If disipline is your problem, there is an absolute answer for you. It comes from a famous shoe manufacturer. The answer is this: JUST DO IT. There is no alternative.

Now that you have read this, here is a question: Does this lesson get added to the long list of things you have read but not acted on or make you sit up and make changes about how you trade for the better? If your problems are apparent after reading this, make the change. Make a business (trading) plan, and monitor the plan and your progress.

In summary, psychological issues make up 85 percent of the trading equation. Discipline is the essence of all of the psychological issues. It permeates throughout the whole process. All the rules and procedures and plans do not matter if they are not followed. There is little doubt that for those who seek an education in trading, that failure rarely comes from writing the wrong plan. Failure comes from not writing a plan at all, or not following the one that is written.

I would like to close with my second favorite quote: "I just wait until there is money lying in the corner and all I have to do is go over there and pick it up. I do nothing in the meantime. In essence, by not wanting to trade, I have inadvertently transformed myself into a master of patience. By forcing myself to wait until there was a trade that appeared so compelling that I could not stand the thought of not taking it, I had vastly improved the odds...." - James Rodgers.

Some of Your Best Qualities...

I ended the last lesson with my second favorite quote. I thought you would like to know my favorite. Naturally, that is what this lesson will be about.

First, let's discuss the title, which is a bit deceiving. "Some of your best qualities may be hurting you." Yes, it is true. Trading is unique in many ways. It is not by accident that many of the people who are drawn to trading are successful people from other walks of life. After all, to trade you need some free capital. Many obtain this from running or selling successful businesses, or from high paying professions. The problem is that trading is unique from most other businesses.

Most of your previous successes in life will likely not be able to help you in trading. The things you have learned are often not transferable. Worse than that, they may be harmful. Take the successful doctor. Every time his stop hits, he decides to add more shares. Why? To the skilled trader, this is a crime. To the doctor, this is a way of life; it is bred into his system. What is he thinking? He is thinking about 'saving the patient'. He is taught that the object of his attention must be saved at all costs, at all measures. To trade, he has to adopt the philosophy of 'killing the patient at the first signs of ill health'. This appalls him at some level.

Consider the skilled lawyer. He is taught to make a case and an argument for any possible situation. As his stock begins to fall, he can come up with dozens of ways to justify the position. He is skilled at making the case and does so for the stock as it begins to fall. 'They just had good news, the fundamentals are excellent, this is just a shake out, and the market makers are playing games'. He will use a thousand different arguments to stay with a loser.

Consider any successful businessman. Often in the beginning, success came by simply working harder. Putting in more hours, taking on more personally. Doing what ever it takes. Unfortunately, trading harder is not even a working concept. Consider the accountant. The accountant is a perfectionist with numbers. The thought of having red ink on a trade can be hard to take. It forms the need to not take small stops, hoping that the ledger can show all winners today.

Consider even the professional athlete. Losing is not an option. Unfortunately, in trading, losing is mandatory. Losing the right way is what matters, small amounts on appropriate trades. Once a trade has stopped, it is a loss and the trader moves on. The trader knows that what matters is the process that delivers winners over a period of time, not what happens on one trade. To the athlete, losing is not acceptable. It must be avoided at all costs and at all levels.

So what is helpful? Learning the whole process of trading. Learning from those who have been through it, or having the ability to learn and adapt quickly as you go. Having the mindset of having a plan, being able to adjust that plan, and carrying out the plan until the results are reached. Then constantly evaluating the process, eliminating mistakes and being mindful of the need to change and be flexible. There is a quote I have always liked and is, in fact, my favorite. I find its application to trading to be unique.

"Nothing in this world can take the place of persistence. Talent will not; nothing is more common than unsuccessful people with talent. Genius will not; unrewarded genius is almost a proverb. Education will not; the world is full of educated derelicts. Persistence and determination alone are omnipotent. The slogan 'press on' has solved and always will solve the problems of the human race."
-Calvin Coolidge

I find this to be a good warning to all. Many talents you have may not directly contribute to your trading. An open mind, coupled with persistence and determination in your goal are keys to successful trading.

The Need to be Right

If you are in the early stages of learning to trade, you will become a compilation of all those you learned from. You will become your own unique breed of trader. We all come to the table with certain expectations and beliefs and with some emotional baggage. We all learn from reading, studying websites, and other traders, some informally, some by paying for education in the form of trading rooms, seminars and mentors. Every time you learn something, it adds to your experience as a trader. Eventually you become the sum of all you have learned. Even if you have a mentor you have tried to emulate, you will never be like your mentor. You will be unique.

While no two traders are identical, most successful traders do share some common characteristics. Most have learned the value of a trading plan. Most have learned the need for stops. Most have learned about discipline. However, it takes a long time to understand the subject of this lesson; the need to be right.

The topic is a simple one. Yet it eludes many traders. It seems only obvious that if we want to be successful, we need to be right in our underlying assumptions. If we want to trade stocks, we should focus on being right about the direction stocks are going. Correct? Well, not really.

Most traders focus too much on their need to be right. This can be detrimental and needs to be addressed. The truth is that we are dealing in the stock market. There is not a system, method or pattern that can produce accurate results all the time. If there were, it would be known to all. All would be using it. Ironically, if this was the case, when everyone started using the system, it could no longer work. A 'catch-22' of sorts, but it just goes to show that it is obvious that there will never be a perfect system or indicator.

The best we can do is to study each situation, collect the evidence, and make a high probability decision at the proper moment. What is of primary importance is how the situation is handled when the trader is right, and how the situation is handled when the trader is wrong. What is the most common reason traders fail? The answer is not following stops. What is another top reason traders fail? The answer is not letting winners run.

Not following a stop is an example of handling the situation improperly when a trader is wrong about the trade. Not letting a trade hit a target is an example of handling the situation improperly when a trader is right about the trade. What good is being right if you don't get paid for it? From the beginning, good traders assume that the trade may go bust. They know how much money they have risked and when they will get out. They will analyze other options, such as profiting from the stock, which is now moving 'against the odds'.

Good traders also know how to balance being right and being timely. I know of an advisory service that is taking credit for having predicted the fall of the Dow. The only problem is that they began that prediction when the Dow hit 6000. Quite a hollow victory. Waiting for too much information may make you right more often, but to what avail? It is like the trader that finally decides the NASDAQ is going higher intraday, because it broke the high of the day. The only problem is that the NASDAQ rallied 30 points to come back to break the high of the day, it is so extended, there is no room left for profit. The trader may be right, but his late decision awards him no money.

Yes, we need to be right a fair amount when we trade. However, if your average winner is three times your average loser, you only need to be right 25 percent of the time to be breaking even gross. Accept that this is not an exact science, and never will be. We are reading people's emotions. Accept that you will be wrong a certain amount of the time and should accept that graciously. Focus on how you handle your winner and loser. Make timely, high probability decisions when you have sufficient evidence, and do so consistently and objectively.

The Ways Traders Learn

The general concept presented here regarding the four steps of learning is not new. It is a concept that has been helpful in understanding the stages we go through in learning. I find it very useful as it applies to learning the art of trading.

The first step is where everyone starts out when learning a new skill like trading. It is called "unconscious incompetence" and it is the most dangerous time. This is the stage where the person who wants to trade has no knowledge of the subject (incompetent), and ever worse, they do not even know what it is they do not know (unconscious). This can lead to quick failure, as frustration comes easily. Have you ever tried learning new software, and after struggling for a while finally gave in and took a course or read a book about the software? Once you know how much there is to learn, you see the need for education and the frustration ends. Unfortunately for many new traders, they never leave the first step. They feel that trading is easy and never seek education. They usually quit early, either out of money or feeling frustrated.

The second step is an important one. It is called "conscious incompetence." It doesn't sound much better; but it is a big step. Here the trader comes to the realization that they need help. They realize that while they may be very educated and successful in past endeavors, it is not helping in the quest to make money trading. Rather than continue unsuccessfully, they turn to someone for help. They finally know that they don't know what to do. The time it takes to become conscious of their incompetence may vary from a couple days to never.

The third step is the long journey and the most time consuming. It is the quest to become "consciously competent." This is the step where the skills are learned to succeed at the task. For the trader, this is the process of learning strategies, money management, discipline, psychology and all the little ins-and-outs of the market. This is the time when they learn to be successful. The time frame here is hard to determine. For some it can be rather quick. For most, even successful traders, it is a process that never stops.

Note, that while success can be enjoyed at this stage, it is happening at a conscious level. That means that every thing that is done needs to be planned, reviewed, and evaluated. Being "consciously competent" means that in order to be competent, you must consciously think about the process at every step. This is why so many fail even when they reach this level. Once success has been had, many turn off the conscious thinking. They then have problems and begin to think that their successes were just luck. This is where the psychological aspects of trading really come in. Here is where those who have the ability to stick to what they have learned, to stick to their plans and to follow up to make sure, really do well.

The next step is the one of true mastery. It is "unconscious competence." It is performing the skill as a pure habit. It is your body and nerves reacting without consulting your brain. Examples are most easily found in professional athletes. Tiger Woods is 'unconsciously competent' at golf. He does not address the ball and start thinking, "Now, let's see, my right hand goes here…" Can one get to this level in trading? It is possible. Very few are. It would require the engrained discipline to never be distracted from your plan. It would mean no matter what trade came along, if it did not meet criteria you have set for yourself, it would not be considered. It would mean that when a trade hit a predefined level, it would be exited without thought or hesitation.

The good news is that you do not have to be at the fourth level to be successful. Many traders may be at the third level their whole career and be just fine. They will only do well however, if they remember that they are at the third level, and that conscious thinking in the form of planning, discipline and follow up are needed every day.

Using Public Fear as a Trading Tool

A part of conscious thinking would be to ask yourself whether a pullback in the market on daily charts is buyable. A long line of bulls all want to be the first one in on the move up. A long line of bears want to know if it is time to cover or is this just a 'technical' bounce.

I have spent a great deal of time and energy using technical analysis to help determine these issues. Many lessons in this book have discussed this. However, many questions often remain. Is this a quality pullback?

Is this really support here? Is the uptrend still in place, or has it been degraded? Trying to determine on a daily or weekly chart when a pullback is buyable is not always an easy task. There are many details that we look to in technical analysis that help make a case either way. I want to touch on one detail that not all traders are familiar with. The use of public fear to measure the realism of a pullback.

This involves the use of measuring the public's view of the market as it is measured by the open interest in puts. Puts are options contracts that go up in value when the underlying security (the NASDAQ market, for example) goes down. The theory is that when much of the general public are buying puts, the market is ready to go up. Some people may consider this 'reverse psychology' or 'the public is always wrong'. Think of it this way. If everyone is bearish, as shown by buying puts, who is left to sell stock? If no one is bearish, as shown by a very low volume of puts being bought, then there are still many holding stocks that will likely be sold in the future if the market comes down more. Or at the very least, they are not going to be new buyers.

There are two measures that help you get a handle on this. One is the Put-Call Ratio (PCRATIO on Real Tick), and the other is the Volatility Index ($VIX.X on Real Tick). Below are charts of the NASDAQ index Figure 4-1), and the VIX (Figure 4-2) and the PC Ratio (Figure 4-3).

The top chart is the NASDAQ index. The question here is, can the Pristine Buy Set-up (see Appendix A) that happened at 2 (Febuary 8) be bought long term? It is a nice looking set-up. The pullback on the weekly chart is 50 percent from the September lows to the January high. We have filled that gap to some support as shown by 1. We have a changing of the guard and the move did provide four partial days of upside. A playable rally, but would you be long in core positions here? We were not because of the next two charts.

The Volatility index moves inverse to the market. It can be used to confirm moves in the market. Notice the rally that ended on Febuary 8

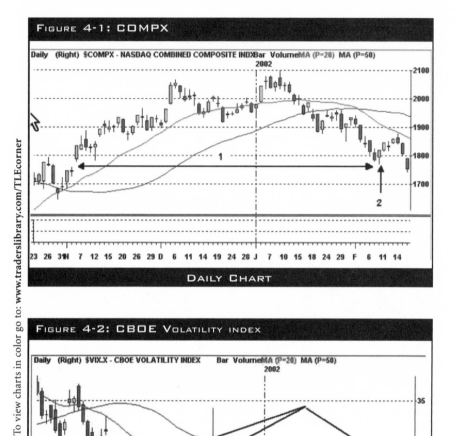

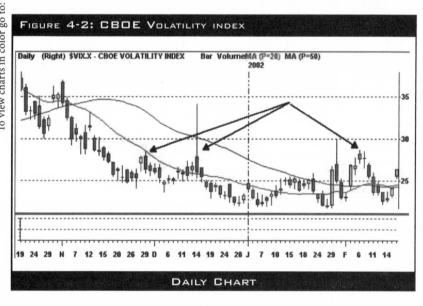

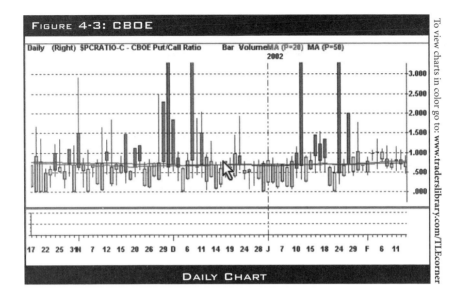

FIGURE 4-3: CBOE

Daily (Right) $PCRATIO-C - CBOE Put/Call Ratio   Bar Volume MA (P=20) MA (P=50)

DAILY CHART

(matching the pullback in the NASDAQ on Febuary 8) did not take out prior highs, as shown by the arrows. Note that the corresponding days in the NASDAQ did produce lower lows that should have been confirmed by higher highs in the Volatility index. This is telling us that there was not much fear in this pullback, that the average investor was still hanging on to stocks, and was not short the market. This is not a good combination to make a buyable long term rally. Note that prior highs from November were well into the 30's.

The next chart does not graph well as the PC ratio usually stays in a tight range; however, I did want to show that a PC ratio over one is generally considered to be getting high enough to show fear amongst investors and show a high level of shorting in the market. Notice that during the Febuary 8 pullback, the PC ratio could not close over the .7-.8 area on average.

Overall, the pullback came in the NASDAQ and as it approached a key level, most investors simply were not selling. They were bullish; there was still much stock to sell. Due more to a lack of buyers and low volume, the pullback did not bring about selling. That means there are less investors needing to buy stock; they already own it.

Another tool to consider in trading is the losing trade. To analyze these types of trades, see the following lesson.

Analysis of a Losing Trade

Many traders spend much time discussing why a trade worked after the fact. How obvious it was once the chart is drawn. I will tell you that all trades do not work out, I don't even expect them to. It is the very nature of trading that trades will fail. As traders, we are just trying to get the odds in our favor with every analysis. Trading is all about getting the odds in your favor. Then, it is how you handle the winners, and how you handle the losers. To always try to improve the odds, we analyze all trades after they are closed, especially the losers to see what, if anything, can be learned.

That being said, I want to share with you an after the trade analysis of a losing trade. The trade was on AT&T Corp. (T) and was intended as a swing trade, with the back half being held as a core trade.

Next is a daily chart of AT&T Corp (Figure 4-4). The following was the rationale for the long position:

1. T had been in a nice uptrend (not shown) since May of this year. This pullback began in October and came down to a major support area from July. This gave us reason to look at the daily chart to find a playable set-up.

2. While the daily chart did not offer a clean set-up for entry, an interesting pattern did form: large volume in mid-October, after falling for a month, large bottoming tails in the area of November 1, and a very nice consolidation in mid-November after the bounce off the lows.

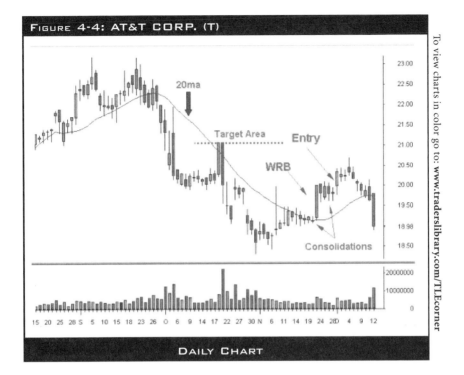

FIGURE 4-4: AT&T CORP. (T)

To view charts in color go to: www.traderslibrary.com/TLEcorner

DAILY CHART

3. While this stock was in a downtrend for the last three months on the daily chart, we were looking for the stock to transition from Stage One to Stage Two because we were in the weekly support area. The test would be the mid-November base. If the downtrend were to continue, this base should be resolved to the downside.

4. The base broke out with a Wide Range Bar (WRB) to the upside. After a four-day consolidation staying in the upper third of the WRB, we played T on the next break out, on December 1 at 19.87. The swing target was just under 21.00, the mid-October high. The stop was under 19.62. We were using a 'core' stop mentality and keeping the stop in place until the daily chart put in a higher low.

The trade went well for four days. It rallied two-thirds of the way to the target before stalling. We expected the pullback to put in a higher low then proceed to the target. The morning of December 11 looked like things were on target. Then T sold off for all-day and closed just above the stop. The next day, T gapped down, and we used 'disaster rules' to manage the exit, which turned out to be more than the stop. Most daily charts do not show this gap down (the above does not), due to the frequent problem with listed stocks showing 'bad ticks' before they open, but T did gap down on the 12th.

Now for the important question: Was there anything to be learned from the set-up of the trade, or the management?

1. A closer look at the weekly chart (Figure 4-5) gives us a chance to see if multiple time frames were coordinated. We especially want to look at the next bigger time frame to make sure it does not conflict with the trade. There were some small signs that this weekly uptrend may not have held that support. The WRB at the end of September was the biggest red bar on the weekly uptrend. This does not mean the uptrend was over, but it is a clue, and that is what we are looking for; to see if there were enough clues to learn to handle a trade like this better.

2. Note the bar labeled A. This is highlighted because that top tail hit as a weekly Pristine Buy Set-up (see Appendix A) in an area that would have maintained the weekly uptrend. This is the area that should have held up. The next bar was another fairly wide bar that actually went a little below support. The stock did bounce from the area of support, but a really strong stock may not have pulled back that far.

3. As far as trade management, a review is needed to see if one's current money management rules were followed, and if they were, to evaluate if there should be changes made. If you find that a rule is consistently not doing its job, you might consider changing the rule to improve future performance. The issue here is should a trade be allowed to go negative after getting that close to a target. As a core trade, the plan was to not raise the stop until a daily pivot point formed.

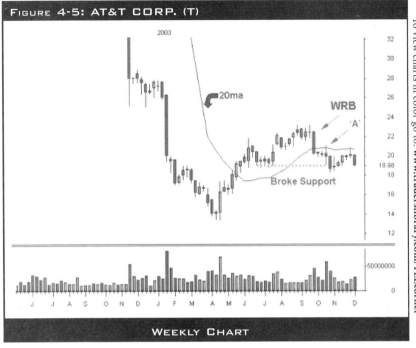

FIGURE 4-5: AT&T CORP. (T)

WEEKLY CHART

4. An issue could be raised that the stock was held when it closed just above the stop the day prior to the trade stopping. The gap down the next morning turned the trade negative.

Here is a summary of what was learned;

1. This trade was a core trade, but the weekly chart was only glanced at and not studied. The daily chart had a very nice set-up, but perhaps the time frame should have stayed swing with smaller targets until more could be learned from the weekly.

2. The management of the trade was not a mistake, as it followed the plan outlined for this type of trade. However, perhaps a change in the plan should be made for a holding that closes just above the stop on a bearish bar, as T did the day before it stopped.

Printing out charts and summarizing all the trades you do should be a part of your regular routine, first to make sure you followed your trading plan, and second, to see if consistent issues arise that would make you change your plan.

Chapter 5
Technical Lessons

Some Common Mistakes

I'd like to think that traders who have read this book so far have learned at least one concept that can help them improve their trading. Sometimes the lessons are big concepts; sometimes they are small points. Some are technically oriented and some are psychologically oriented. Today I would like to focus on what I feel are the two most common mistakes traders make.

The categorization that they are the most *common mistakes* is subjective on my part. It comes from running the Pristine Method® Trading Room and dealing with the many interesting questions traders ask. I feel that if all traders were aware of these two issues, it would immediately help their trading.

The first one is a simple concept, but so common that it takes first place in my mind as the most deadly mistake. The mistake is this: Traders want to short strong stocks (or buy weak ones) without any particular strategy other than the stock appears over extended.

Trading does involve some subjectivity. It is hard to eliminate. However, the more you can limit this and stay objective, the better off your trading will be. Calling a stock 'extended' without any objective criteria is difficult. It is difficult to do even with objective criteria. The truth is that most traders would be better served by staying with the trend. Going against the trend has serious limitations. Experienced traders will look at the relationship of the price to moving averages, how the volume is entering the stock, and often 'zoom down' to refine an entry. Even after all this, these are low odds trades.

Why are traders so drawn to these since there are so many drawbacks? Simple. The home-run. Somewhere, somehow, sometime the trader saw, read about, or perhaps actually shorted a stock at its high, and caught a big move. It can happen. When it does, all the trader remembers is that great trade and not all the failures on similar set-ups since then. Try tracking your results and see how much money you actually make fighting the trend. It may surprise you.

Consider the cheetah. It is the fastest land animal. When hunting for dinner, it could catch any elk it wanted to. However, the cheetah will always go after the slowest elk, the one with the limp. It may not be glamorous, but the cheetah eats every day.

So what is the second most common mistake? Shorting multiple bar drops to support (or buying multiple bar rallies to resistance) because it appears that the support (or resistance) level is now 'broken'. This one is a bit more complicated, so I have included a chart. See the daily chart of MCHP, below (Figure 5-1).

Note here that the bar labeled WRB is the bar in debate. Traders always want to short this bar when it breaks the support level to the left, signified by the green dots.

First of all, support areas (this applies to resistance as well) are concepts, not exact numbers. They are 'rubber bands' not glass plates. How you approach the support is more important than if you 'break' the magic number. Notice that the WRB is the sixth day down when it begins. Then MCHP falls more than it has on any day on this chart. Now do you want to short this stock? The smart trades were short much earlier, and as the

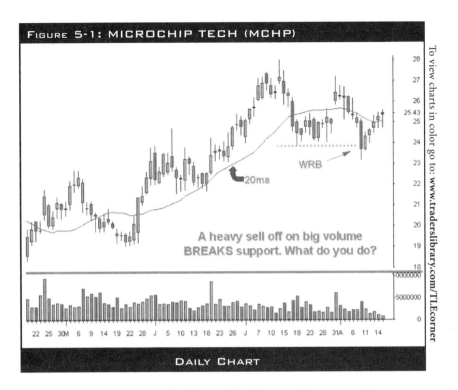

FIGURE 5-1: MICROCHIP TECH (MCHP)

WRB

20ma

A heavy sell off on big volume
BREAKS support. What do you do?

To view charts in color go to: www.traderslibrary.com/TLEcorner

DAILY CHART

stock loses momentum to the downside, these traders are ready to cover. Add to that, the trader who mistakenly does short this on the last day, and you get this result; lots of people who need to buy this stock, driving the price up.

Now, no one is saying that this stock is not damaged on the long side. No one is saying that it may not be a nice short after a small weak rally. It is, however, a very low odds play as a short when it goes below the prior lows on the daily. Good traders will not only avoid this, but profit from the move to the long side.

Track your trades and see if this makes an improvement to your bottom line.

Was That a Double Top?

You do not have to be trading long before the term "double top" or "double bottom" is heard. What constitutes a double top/bottom and can this be used in your trading?

Like all of trading, and all of technical analysis, nothing is written in stone in terms of what direction a stock will go. As traders, all we try to do is to put the odds in our favor whenever we can. With that in mind, let's take a look at some issues to consider when you think you see a double top forming. Also keep in mind that this discussion, like most discussions of charts, applies to all time frames. You can use this information on a 5-minute chart for intraday plays or on a daily for swing and core plays.

Let's talk about double bottoms. This discussion will apply equally as well to double tops if you change the appropriate wording (high instead of low, etc.) Any time a stock approaches the area of a prior low, it is a potential double bottom. Any prior low offers some support and is likely to cause the stock to at least hesitate the decline. It may then hold as a sideways consolidation (base). Or it may rally, but only to later return to the low (dare I say, a 'triple' bottom?) Or, it may produce a substantial rally, challenging prior highs. Or, it may rally so strong that the bottom becomes a major low for a long time to come. The question becomes; which of these possibilities is likely to happen? Do you play the double bottom long for a scalp, long for a long trade, or dare I say, anticipate the short by shorting the rally from the potential double bottom?

Here is the checklist of things you will want to examine to determine how your stock will react to a potential double bottom. The list looks long, but after a while many of these things will be second nature to you.

1. What was the prior trend of the stock? If the stock is in a downtrend, it is more likely that the double bottom will not hold (or a double top will hold). This means that a stock that is in a downtrend is likely to continue the downtrend and most prior lows will be ignored, or produce small bounces that are likely

to be shortable bounces. If the stock is in an uptrend, and the stock is pulling back to a prior low, it is more likely the double bottom will hold (double top would fail) and the uptrend will continue.

2. What is the relative strength compared to the market in general, or the sector the stock is in? Let's take an intraday example. Let's say you use the NASDAQ futures contract to represent the market. Let's say your stock is in an uptrend and has pulled back to a potential double bottom. Let's say the futures continue trading lower and take out the days low. Your stock continues holding. If the futures get bullish, it is more likely that the stock will move off the bottom and produce a strong double bottom and potential bullish move. Take the reverse example and it will be even clearer. Let's say the same stock is sitting on a potential double bottom while the futures are rallying hard. The futures rally into a resistance area and your stock barely moves off the bottom. It is weak and not likely to hold the bottom when the futures pullback.

3. Where are the major moving averages? Identifying a 200 period moving average is a good way to help confirm the trend of the stock. Above the 200 confirms a strong stock, below confirms weak, which can help in determining the answer to question #1. Using the 20 period moving average (MA) can help you determine when a stock has moved too far in one direction. A 'return' to the 20 MA can indicate that the prior trend is now ready to resume. For example, a strong stock that has just pulled back to a prior low is more likely to hold as a double bottom if it is now meeting the rising 20 MA. A potential double bottom that hits the rising 20 MA is a good combination for the stock to continue up. Conversely, a stock that rallies up to the 20 MA and then quickly returns to the prior low is not as likely to hold as a double bottom.

4. What is the measured amount of the last bounce compared to prior moves? Picture a stock on the daily chart that has been basing (consolidating) for days. It breaks down and falls 8 points, puts in a low, and then bounces 2 points. It then rolls over and goes back to challenge the low. Another potential double bottom. This stock would not be as likely to hold. It would be more likely to head lower. Why? After an 8 point drop, a 2 point 'bounce' is only a 25% retracement. That is not a sign of strength, even weak stocks should be able to retrace 30-40% of the last move. Stronger stocks will do over 50%. Naturally some will do 100%. What if a stock does not even bounce, and simply 'bases' along the low or a prior low? It is likely the weakest sign of all. However you must look at the other criteria as well.

For example, a stock is in a downtrend on a 5-minute chart. It is below its 200 MA. On the last move, it dropped 2 points without much relief. It is well below the 20 MA at this point and begins to move up. It rallies a half point into the declining 20 MA and rolls over and returns to the prior low. It does all this while the futures have been relatively strong, a potential double bottom. This is one that is not likely to hold. I have used the above criteria to create a scenario that is least likely to produce a bullish bounce. It is most likely to be a short, not a long.

On the other hand, picture a stock that has been in an uptrend on the 5-minute chart. It is above its 200 MA. The stock moves up in the morning and sets up a sideways base. It moves up another half point, and then returns to the base. As it returns to the base (potential double bottom), it meets the rising 20 MA. All this happens while the futures have been pulling back hard from an early uptrend. When the futures find their footing, this stock is the most likely to act bullishly off of the double bottom.

All of the above comments apply equally as well for double tops, if you change the appropriate wording. For example, picture a stock that has been in a downtrend on the 5- minute chart. It is below its 200 MA. The stock moves down in the morning and sets up a sideways base. It moves down a half point, and then returns to the base. As it returns to the base (potential double top), it meets the falling 20 MA. All this happens while the futures have been rallying hard from an early downtrend. When the futures resume selling off, this stock is the most likely to act bearishly off of the double top.

Let's take a look at how these concepts apply on some real charts (Figures 5-2 and 5-3).

Notice in the example below that on August 14, Microsoft (Figure 5-2) opened neutral and started a small downtrend on the 5-minute chart. This downtrend was a continuation of the prior days downtrend. At 11:00 AM the stock made a new low for the day and sound support at 65.2. Notice the stock made not a double, not a triple, but a quadruple bottom over the next 2 hours (points A, B, C, D). Many would say that a quadruple bottom must be a sign of strength! Take a look at the guidelines

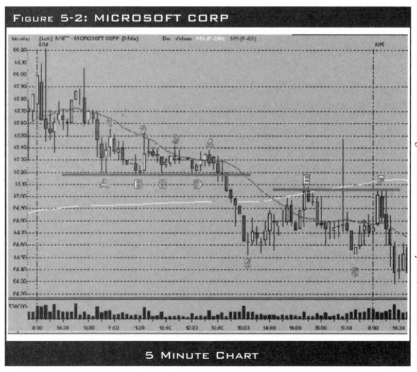

FIGURE 5-2: MICROSOFT CORP

5 MINUTE CHART

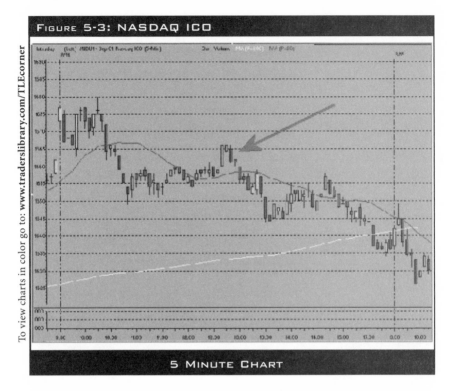

FIGURE 5-3: NASDAQ ICO

5 MINUTE CHART

above, it was not hard to predict that MSFT would head lower (that is to say, the double or multiple bottom failed) for the following reasons.

First, the stock was in a downtrend going into this time period. Since the opening, MSFT formed lower highs and lower lows. The trend is likely to continue. Second, compare the chart from 11:00 until 2:00 with the NASDAQ futures (Figure 5-3). Notice that the futures during this time period had higher lows and broke to the upside at 12:45. During this time period, MSFT did nothing bullish. When the futures returned to their original base, MSFT quickly broke down. Third, notice the declining 20 MA on the MSFT chart. It is in red. It held as an almost perfect downtrend line, containing every bounce by MSFT during this time period. Finally, notice the bounces off of the bottom every time, shown by numbers 1, 2, 3, and 4. Notice the first bounce, from A to 1 went from about 65.2 to 65.55. That is .35, and the original fall was from about 66.1 to 65.2. The retracement stayed well under half of the original fall.

Apply these same steps to see if you can predict the outcome of the successful double top from E to F. A successful double top has a bearish outcome, just like a failed double bottom has a bearish outcome. First, the stock was in a downtrend again. Second, the futures action was not helpful in this case. The futures actually weakened so much that it contributed to the fall of MSFT the next morning. Relative strength was strong and could have led to a break out if the futures would have held better. However, check the third item; the powerful 200 period moving average (in white) came up on top of the prices, (that is to say the price fell below the powerful 200 MA), which was an important item in the double top holding. Fourth, notice the bounce from E to 6. It was a 100 percent retracement of the move going into point E, from 5 to E. This means that the top is strong and the next challenge of the top is likely to fail.

Knowing about double tops and bottoms will help support your trading plan.

Support and Resistance

Let's start with some definitions. In my book, *Tools and Tactics for the Master Day Trader*, I define support as "a price level or area at which the demand for a stock will likely overwhelm the existing supply and halt the current decline." Resistance is defined as "a price level or area at which the supply for a stock will likely overwhelm the existing demand and halt the current advance."

Note that the words 'or area' are part of the definition. This is the first point I want to make. Support and resistance are not broken by a one penny violation. They are areas. Think of them as rubber bands, not glass plates. Note also that the time frame matters also. A ten cent violation of a 7 dollar stock on a 2 minute chart may be a major violation. However, a 50 cent violation of the 200 period moving average on a daily chart on QCOM may be nothing. It is very relative. From here on out, for simplicity, I will discuss support though all the concepts, apply in reverse for resistance. The charts presented here are all the same chart, a daily of the NASDAQ Composite, the COMPX, with a 20 and 50 period moving average.

Notice in figure 5-4 that I have identified a form of support. A rising moving average. Several times the COMPX found support and rallied off of the rising 20 period moving average. When this moving average is no longer serving as support, it may be time to open a new play book. Notice that the break of the 20 MA comes after a pullback, so good traders don't short there necessarily, but the next rally is watched to see how it reacts.

You will see examples of support found on a rising trend line in figure 5-5.

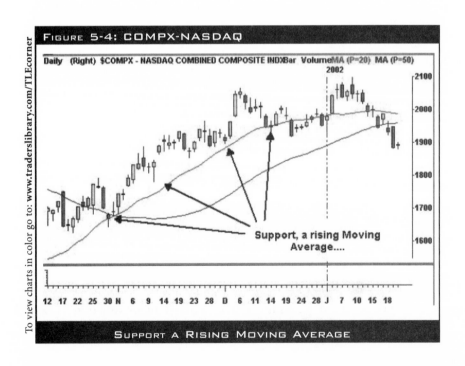

FIGURE 5-4: COMPX-NASDAQ

Daily (Right) $COMPX - NASDAQ COMBINED COMPOSITE INDXBar VolumeMA (P=20) MA (P=50)

Support, a rising Moving Average....

SUPPORT A RISING MOVING AVERAGE

124

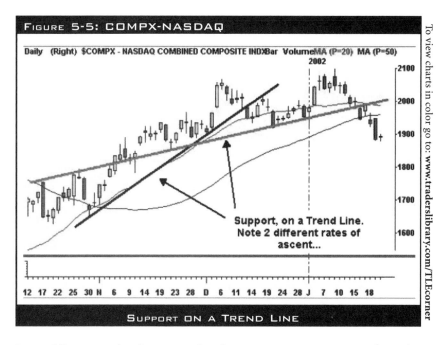

FIGURE 5-5: COMPX-NASDAQ

Daily (Right) $COMPX - NASDAQ COMBINED COMPOSITE INDXBar VolumeMA (P=20) MA (P=50)

Support, on a Trend Line. Note 2 different rates of ascent...

SUPPORT ON A TREND LINE

A trend line must be drawn on the chart to represent an area of consistently rising lows. While there is an art to drawing these, for now you can see how this concept works and how the trend line can often be similar to a moving average.

Next we have some examples of major and minor support, forming horizontal support lines (Figure 5-6).

Note also that there is what we call major and minor support. Major support is a pullback to a prior low to re-test that area. Minor support is formed by a pullback to test a prior high.

In the first chart above, notice the base that formed at the end of November. The pullback on December 20 was a test of minor support, the high of that base. Later, on January 16, the test was a re-test of that low area, so it was major support.

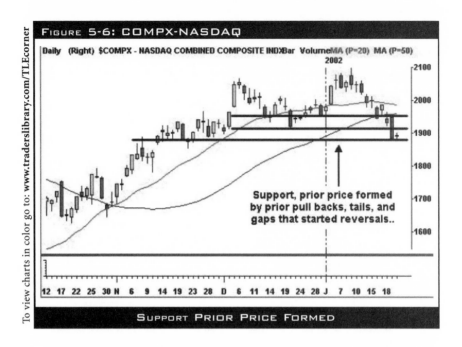

Notice these two areas. First they are areas, not exact numbers. Notice one support area produces a bounce to new highs. The next one bounced one day and failed. That is important.

So what good is this if you can't nail down support to a single penny, and if sometimes they fail? Isn't trading supposed to be fool proof? Well, it is when we get in an area of support than we open up our playbook of bullish strategies and wait for those strategies entries to hit. That is why we teach strategies, and why they all have specific entries and stops and targets.

We take the plays that have good entries and proper stops. This lets the trades that work give good results, and the ones that don't have small losses. The reverse is of course for resistance and bearish plays. It tells you the time and area that you should look in order to use the strategies that you have learned to trust.

That First Pullback

This will be a very simple yet powerful lesson. It is one you can begin using immediately. You may have heard of this concept but perhaps are not aware of the simple power it holds. It is a concept taught throughout Pristine. In the seminar, we go into great detail about handling the stages of the market. After that, we discuss the advanced topic of how to handle the transitions that occur to lead from one stage into another. Understanding the transitions can lead to the highest degree of market mastery. While there is much to comprehend in this area, I would like to show you two examples of how to handle a transition from a sideways consolidation to an uptrend.

These are both examples of using what we refer to as 'buy point number two'. This is the safest (though not always the best) buy point. Let's take a look at the 5-minute chart of Novavax Inc. (NVAX), (Figure 5-7).

NVAX has a potential buy set-up on the daily chart. We were looking to buy over the prior days high, as shown by the red line. While I decided this pattern on the daily was strong enough to play over the prior day's high, I had some concerns about this entry because: 1.) the daily chart was not perfect on the pullback and 2.) the play was hitting in-between reversal times. I am a big believer in reversal times. This play hit a couple minutes after 9:45 AM. The answer for those wanting to be more conservative was to wait for the first pullback and analyze how it looks.

The pullback came at 10:20 AM and was a very nice Pristine Buy Set-up (see Appendix A) on the 5-minute chart. It had a bottoming tail (BT), formed at minor support (MS), the green line at the rising 20-period moving average (20ma), had the proper retracement form where the rally began (40/60), happened at reversal time (RT) and had relative strength to the market (RS). Also, by playing this buy set-up, the stop could be used under the bottoming tail, providing a tight stop. Those who took

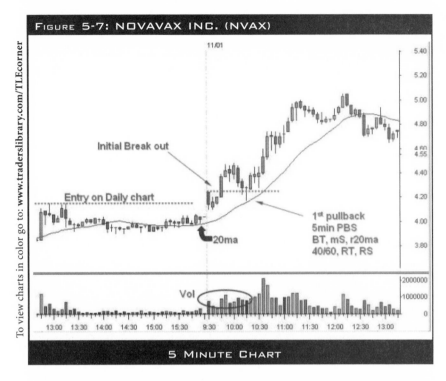

FIGURE 5-7: NOVAVAX INC. (NVAX)

11/01

Initial Break out

Entry on Daily chart

20ma

1st pullback
5min PBS
BT, mS, r20ma
40/60, RT, RS

Vol

5 MINUTE CHART

that move aggressive entry over the high of the day had the option of adding on this pullback and raising the stop to the same bottoming tail.

So, if the aggressive entry worked in this case, why all the fuss about waiting for the first pullback? Here is why. It often keeps you out of a play that fails to follow through. From the same day, look at the chart of Broadcom Corp (Figure 5-8).

BRCM had been pulling back on the daily and was in a weekly support area. The pullback on the 5-minute chart this morning produced a nice rally that filled the gap and then based in the upper half of that move. This base looked like it would move the stock higher and a 'breakout' happened at 1:30 reversal time. However, this stock was still in downtrends on all intraday charts except the 5-minutes. So the 'safety' provided by the first pullback made sense. After the 'breakout', the next bar retraced 100 percent of the move. Not a bullish sign. Compare this to

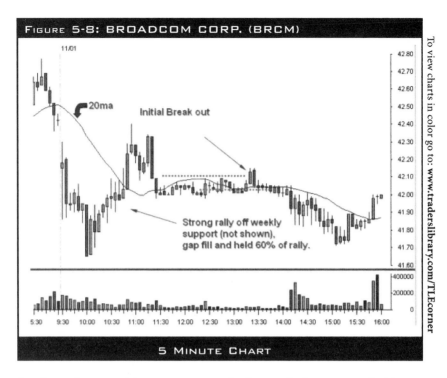

To view charts in color go to: www.traderslibrary.com/TLEcorner

the chart above and how NVAX acted. The stock then proceeded lower without ever forming a buy set-up, so we were able to stay out and avoid a stop out.

When in doubt, consider the safety provided by waiting for the first pullback.

Recognizing a Trend Day

The market gaps up one morning and then just goes sideways all day. The next time the market makes a significant gap up it sells off all day. The next time, after gapping up a huge amount, the market continues to grind up all day long, not even giving a reasonable pullback to enter long. This last scenario is what we call a "trend day."

Knowing which of these scenarios is going to happen is every trader's goal. How can you tell with certainty what will happen? Just like every thing in trading, you can't know for sure. However, there are things to look for that can give you good odds to take higher probability entries. That is, after all, what trading is all about, correct?

On October 14, 2004, we were very bearish from the open. I felt enough information was there to play the day as a 'trend day'.

The first place to look was the daily chart. Below is a daily chart of the SPY, which is the tracking stock of the S&P 500 (Figure 5-9).

In the beginning of October, the SPY made a very bullish move. Noted on the chart is a professional gap (Pro Gap) and bullish wide range bar (+WRB) that took the SPY over the prior high from mid-September. The bulls presumed that the next pullback was buyable, and on October 12, a pullback came that filled the gap and rested on the uptrend line. The next day, the market gapped up, and the bulls assumed it was off to the races. The SPY sold off the entire day. At close that day, there was no support

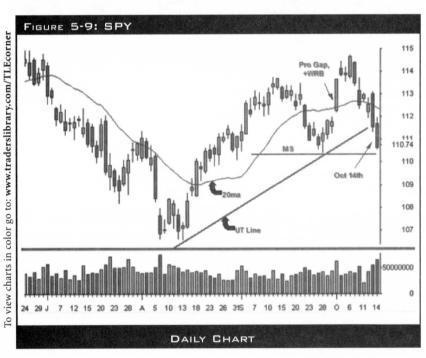

To view charts in color go to: www.traderslibrary.com/TLEcorner

FIGURE 5-9: SPY

DAILY CHART

130

to be seen until the prior low, which was major support (MS). On the morning of the 14th, the day we are analyzing, you can see on the daily chart that the SPY gapped up a little, but it was very small penetration into the large red candle.

Let's take a look at how the day looked on an intraday chart. Below is the SPY for October 14 on a 15-minute chart (Figure 5-10).

Here we can see the pattern that developed on the day prior, the 13th. The market sold off to its lows by 2:00 EST, the last two hours it based. There was not even an attempt to rally back, and the two-hour base gave the market the rest it needed. At open on the 14th, the SPY gapped up a small amount, still inside the tight base provided the last two hours on the 13th. A rally attempt developed and tried to trade over that base. It was immediately sold into, as seen by the topping tail (TT). This happened right at 10:30, which is also important (see prior lesson regarding Reversal Times in Chapter 2). The next bars broke below the base and

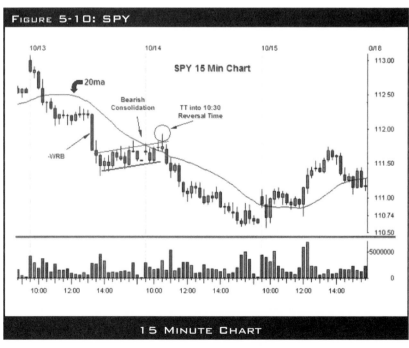

FIGURE 5-10: SPY

there was no support to be seen. This is known as a 'price void', and the support from the prior daily low drew prices down to that area. Through the day, all rallies were shortable and there was a very consistent pattern of selling.

How about some confirming indicators? A very bearish pattern developed in a key sector this same day. The SMH chart below is the tracking stock of the semi-conductors (Figure 5-11).

This is a 15-minute chart covering the same time period as the SPY. Note that the SMH actually gapped down under the base and the rally back was so weak it could not even fill the gap. This is shown by the topping tail (TT) that comes short of filling the gap. This is very bearish and the SMH is a key sector to watch. The SMH led the market down throughout the year and also led the September rally. The SMH is always key to the NASDAQ and therefore, to the broader market. It is hard to mount a rally without the semi-conductors.

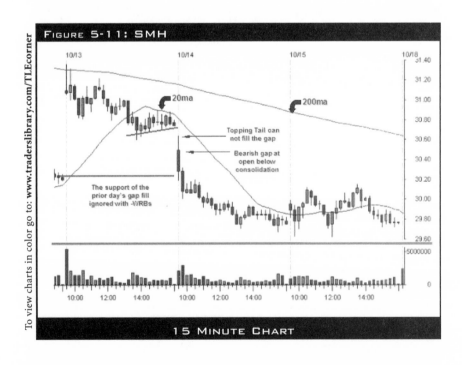

Also, not shown here, is the TRIN for that day. The TRIN is a measure of selling pressure and we use it as a market internal to measure the strength of the market. It is charted inversely, so a move up is bearish. The TRIN moved up during the first bar, to over 1.0, which is bearish, and held an uptrend or sideways base all day. This confirmed selling pressure.

While the average day is filled with many turns and surprises, a careful review of multiple timeframes, gap analysis, and market internals can help get the odds in your favor. Recognizing a 'trend day' when it occurs is one way to do that. Another way is to pay attention to multiple time frames, which are discussed in the next lesson.

The Perspective of Multiple Time Frames

The concept of handling multiple time frames is a very important topic for traders to learn. It is necessary for all traders to understand this idea, as it affects trading at all levels.

All the charts presented in this lesson are to analyze the market one morning as seen through the NASDAQ 100 Trust (QQQQ). We are looking at the implications of a morning breakdown and the expected follow through for the morning and the rest of the day.

From what we can see in this chart (Figure 5-12), the 10:00 decline broke today's low of the day and some support from the end of yesterday. Is this as short as a scalp? Based on what is seen on this chart, some support has been broken. It is not enough to see 'some' support broken. We need to see more of this chart or the chart of the next higher time frame (5-minute, 15-minute) to analyze the trend and other support levels. While in a sense, there may be enough here to justify a 'micro-scalp', how does the trader know if this is a micro-scalp, half-day trade, day trade, or even more? A key to remember is that a 'scalp' is a time frame, not a strategy. I will often hear traders try to justify an ill-conceived play by hiding behind the rationalization that it is a scalp. A bad trade taken for a shorter period of time is still a bad trade.

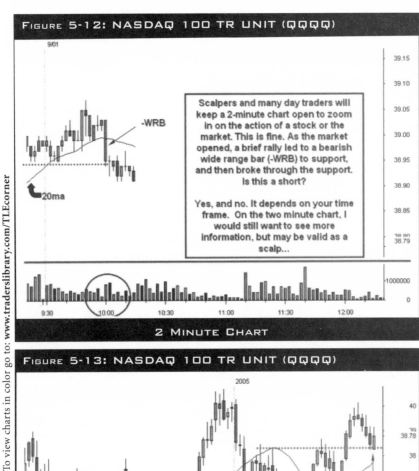

FIGURE 5-12: NASDAQ 100 TR UNIT (QQQQ)

-WRB

20ma

Scalpers and many day traders will keep a 2-minute chart open to zoom in on the action of a stock or the market. This is fine. As the market opened, a brief rally led to a bearish wide range bar (-WRB) to support, and then broke through the support. Is this a short?

Yes, and no. It depends on your time frame. On the two minute chart, I would still want to see more information, but may be valid as a scalp...

2 MINUTE CHART

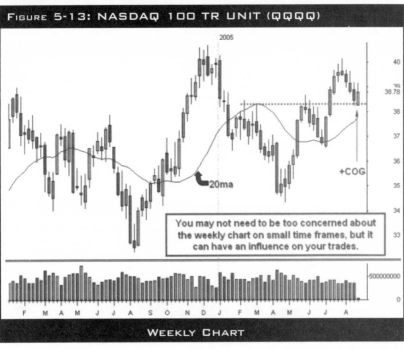

FIGURE 5-13: NASDAQ 100 TR UNIT (QQQQ)

20ma

+COG

You may not need to be too concerned about the weekly chart on small time frames, but it can have an influence on your trades.

WEEKLY CHART

To view charts in color go to: www.traderslibrary.com/TLEcorner

The key here is not to assume more from this breakdown than what this 2-minute chart has to offer. The problem is that many day traders focus so intensely on a 2-minute chart, they lose sight of the bigger picture.

Let's look at how the other time frames come together on this one. First, I want to jump way to the other extreme, the weekly chart (Figure 5-13). Is the weekly necessary for analyzing a true scalp? No. Why show it here? I always start from the top down and it may have some influence on your daily bias.

Here we see the big picture. We appear to be in the beginning of a Pristine Buy Set-up (see Appendix A) on the weekly chart. The bullish bias will carry down to the daily chart and may influence your daily bias. While it is not relevant to analyze the scalp part of the 2-minute chart, it can be relevant in our bias for the rest of the day. For what it is worth, we pick up a bullish daily bias from the weekly.

Now, let's get to the chart with some real influence for a day trader; the hourly (60-minute) chart (Figure 5-14).

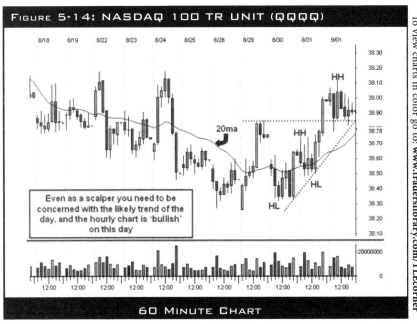

Here we pick up some key information. When day trading, you do not want to be against the hourly trend for long. Until 8/30/05, the hourly had been in a downtrend for quite a while. We see for the most part, lower pivot highs, lower pivot lows, trend lines pointing down, and price staying under the declining 20 period moving average (d20ma) most of the time. On 8/30/05 that higher low led to a series of higher highs (HH) and higher lows (HL) and a rally above the d20ma. The consolidation that formed on 9/01/05, which is the day in question, was bullish. This gave us a bias of wanting to be on the long side for the day, but the hourly chart is doing little to help us see a possible 'entry' to that long side. So, enter the 15-minute chart (Figure 5-15).

Here, things begin to come clear. We enter this chart knowing that the bigger time frames will keep us with a bullish bias. Now we have action-able areas. We can see that the original 2-minute breakdown that began has enough room to fall to be an acceptable scalp, due to the extended

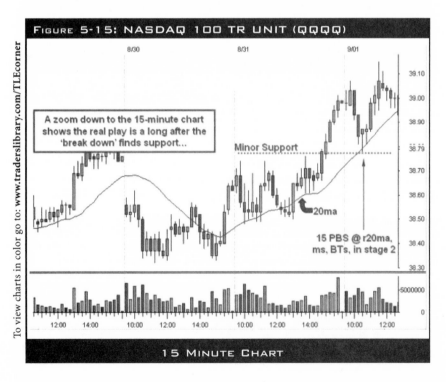

FIGURE 5-15: NASDAQ 100 TR UNIT (QQQQ)

A zoom down to the 15-minute chart shows the real play is a long after the 'break down' finds support...

Minor Support

20ma

15 PBS @ r20ma, ms, BTs, in stage 2

15 MINUTE CHART

move on the hourly and 15-minute charts. We also see a clear target area, the minor support offered by the 'triple topping tail' highs on 8/31/05. As we hit this area, a very clean 15-minute Pristine Buy Set-up (PBS) forms right at a 10:30 reversal time. The PBS is at minor support, with bottoming tails, right around a 50% retracement and right at the r20ma. This rally takes us to a new daily high and our job it done.

In summary, the original 2-minute breakdown was acceptable as a short scalp only because we had enough of a support area broken and there was an extended move up that left a clear void of demand and the next support area was far enough away to justify the play. The real play for the day trader was patience in waiting for reversal time, and a clean set-up in a clear demand area.

Zoom, Zoom, Zoom

"Zoom" is short for zooming down. It is a term we use that refers to going down one timeframe to find an alternate entry to a play. For example, on a daily chart swing trade you go down to the hourly chart to find an entry. This alternate entry could be one that occurs after the larger time frame (daily in this case) entry hits, and you are playing the first pullback. It can also be used before the larger time frame hits. In this case it would be called 'anticipatory' because you are entering before the real play even hits.

There are advantages and disadvantages in doing this. (Isn't that always the case?) In general, anytime you go down a time frame for an entry, you are looking to improve the reward-to-risk one way or another. The disadvantage is that you may enter a play early (when anticipating) that never should have been entered, so you suffer a stop that you would not have, had you waited. Or, when playing the first pullback, you may miss the play entirely, as the stock may never pullback.

Which is best? Well, it depends. It revolves around your intentions and style. Many people often zoom down too much and miss the play, to their detriment. If they wait for the first pullback, it never comes or they can't find the entry. If they anticipate, they stop out on their smaller time frame, but the play succeeds on the bigger one, the one they should have been playing.

If your trading plan requires you to be involved in serious swing trades, it is usually best to play them by the book. It will also revolve around how you feel about having to enter the same trade 2-3 times when stopped out at the first attempts. Some people can't do that from a psychological point of view, some accounts can't afford the extra commissions. This is sometimes required when zooming down. Some people take the attitude that 'legging' into a swing trade during the day and holding it if it is doing well is the way to go. Here, a zoomed down entry is the answer.

Here is an example of a 'triple zoom'. Why would you do this? It may be used as just a great way to align multiple time frames. As in the example below, perhaps you are not even interested in the swing trade. But what better day trade is there than one that is in a swing trade mode?

See the daily chart of Portable Player, Inc. (Figure 5-16). It was set up as a possible swing trade on the last day shown. It had some positive attributes as a swing. The daily was in a pretty nice stage two. It was at the rising 20 period moving average. It had just broken to new highs on the last rally. Some of you may notice some possible problems. It retraced well over 50% of the last rally. It negated all of a powerful breakout bar. Swing tradable? Well, if you're not sure, let's see if we can 'test' an entry to see how it plays out. Notice the topping tail that formed on the last bar of this daily chart? Not all topping tails are bad things. When I see a topping tail develop, I want to see how it forms.

Next is the hourly chart for the same time period (Figure 5-17). Note that here we see that topping tail on the daily, as a nice rally and bullish pullback. The retracement is well under 50% because the real move started the prior day. It sat above the newly rising 20 period moving average. The pullback was controlled. The Pristine Buy-Set-up (see Appendix A) that

FIGURE 5-16: PORTABLE PLAYER INC. (PLAY)

Minor Support

20ma

PBS with BT and hit
yesterday, TT = look
at hourly...

DAILY CHART

FIGURE 5-17: PORTABLE PLAYER INC. (PLAY)

20ma

Hourly PBS his,
partly on gap. The
TT again, look to the
5-minute...

60 MINUTE CHART

formed hit on the gap up in the morning, but after the gap up, there was a pullback allowing for a 30-minute high type of entry. Note that the stop here is much smaller than using the daily chart. Note also the trade off of using the hourly chart. It is possible that play could trade under the stop on the hourly PBS (under the low of the low of the second to last bar, around 27.25) but then recover and be a successful trade. The hourly chart player would out, and the daily chart player would still be in.

Now, let's take a look at that morning pullback on this hourly chart. Look how the pullback looks on a 5-minute chart (Figure 5-18).

On the 5-minute chart, you can see how the hourly topping tail formed. A quick move up for one 5-minute bar (a common sight, remember 9:35 is a reversal time) and then a nice pullback to fill the gap, and a 5-minute Pristine Buy Set-up (PBS) right at 10:00 reversal time. The stop on this play is about $.15 - $.20. Yes, we are looking at playing a nice 5-minute

FIGURE 5-18: PORTABLE PLAYER INC. (PLAY)

5 min PBS at Reversal Time (RT) at r20ma just above gap fill...

20ma

5 MINUTE CHART

PBS that is happening on the pullback of a nice hourly PBS that is happening on the pullback of a nice daily PBS! Is the application real? Yes, very. As I mentioned, there are two uses. First, as a scalper, a five-minute PBS that has the other time frames behind it can help drive the play. You can see the reaction on the 5-minute chart. Second, while zooming down twice may be a bit much for the swing trader, I would be lying if I said this wasn't done. You can play a large lot size with the tight stop of this play, and sell two lots intraday for profit, keeping the number of shares appropriate for you to hold as a swing. Then, if the swing trade does not work, you are more than likely profitable on the whole trade.

Daily Pivot Points

When you look back at daily charts of stocks or indices, they will always have certain things in common. Most stocks will spend the majority of their time trading in a sloppy, non-directional pattern. You will always find some trends, and you will always find key areas on the chart that set significant highs or lows that last for weeks or months. This lesson is about finding those key areas and capitalizing on them.

When stocks are in a nice trend, a consistent pattern develops. These are the ones that we like to trade the most. They have a clean uptrend, or a clean downtrend, or even a clean sideways trend. After all, there are only three ways a stock can trend, correct? By clean, I mean that the bars on the chart tend to follow support and resistance lines (major, minor, or a trend line), they respect moving averages in a consistent way, and continue in the same direction for long periods of time. The bars do not overlap, nor are there spaces between them (both of these caused by gaps).

What happens when the stock breaks tradition? Changes trend? Falls abruptly then reverses? Many of the patterns we know become worthless. Is all lost? No. I teach concepts regarding guerrilla tactics, and concepts regarding Wide Range Bars, Gaps, and failed expectations that can help.

Strategies for Profiting on Every Trade

These concepts can help you do what most say cannot be done. That is, to pick short term to medium term tops and bottoms with amazing accuracy. Let's take a look at the chart below (Figure 5-19).

Generally speaking, the MCHP daily chart is in an uptrend, as shown by higher highs and higher lows. Since we are in an uptrend, I simply identified the long-term bottoms that were formed. These are arrows A, B, and C. Were these areas playable? Let's take a look.

Arrow A is a guerrilla tactic I teach. It is called a Bullish 20-20 play. The key to the formation is that last big red bar just before the arrow. The stock had six lower highs, and then had the largest sell-off (red) bar in recent history. This is a Wide Range Bar (WRB) or a 20/20 Bar (meaning less than 20% tails), which sets up the play. This happens on increased volume. The stock opened flat the next day and the strategy is to go long over the high of the day after 30-minutes of trading. This sets a low that has not been violated to date. Besides being a viable trade, this was a high volume guerrilla tactic that changed the short-term direction of the daily chart.

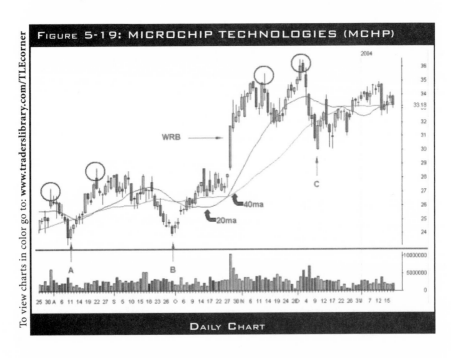

FIGURE 5-19: MICROCHIP TECHNOLOGIES (MCHP)

DAILY CHART

Let's look at arrow B. This is a guerrilla tactic I called a Minor Bullish Mortgage Play. The pullback going into B is starting to look bearish. We were not able to stay above the moving averages, and the pullback challenges the prior low. Going into B, we have 4 lower highs (6 out of 7 also). Then a WRB forms again (not as big as some, which is why this is labeled 'minor'). Then the stock gaps open at or above the high of the prior days bar. Note that MCHP closed at the bottom of that red bar, then opens the next day near the top. The stock sets a higher low, which has not been violated to date.

Next we have arrow C, another guerilla tactic known as a Bullish Gap and Snap Play. Again, five days down followed by a Bearish (red) WRB. This time the stock gaps down, setting up the long entry as the stock penetrates the low of the prior day (or sometimes a 5-minute high if it is a Gap and Snap Plus Play). Again, MCHP sets a higher low, which has not been violated to date. Look at the increased volume at the low. Once again, a high volume guerrilla tactic that changed the short-term direction of the daily chart.

There are so many other points to be made. Look at the tops. Remember, the general trend is up, so we are not looking for major chart changing reversal at the top. However, notice how all the pullbacks start with a Topping Tail after a multiple bar run. These are the four circles. Notice the WRB breakout that is never challenged. There are many other valuable clues. One of them, staying with the trend, is discussed in the next lesson.

Fighting the Trend

You will hear many famous quotes while learning to trade. None will be more enduring than "The trend is your friend." All successful traders know to stay with the trend 92% of the time. That 8%, when a trader fights the trend, is only on a climactic set-up. The climactic set-up has a very firm set of rules that must be followed to play and one of the rules is that a retracement target is used, not a 'new high or low.'

This article is not about the climactic set-up. Rather than explain a strategy that you should only use eight percent of the time, I would like to explain why you should stay with the trend 92% of the time.

First, is the concept that trends tend to stay in place until a shocking occurrence happens or the bigger time frame comes into conflict. The second reason is just a matter of simple math. Since we are not trying to catch the absolute highs and lows, we are trying to take the meat out of any move, that easy part in the middle. If a stock moves twice the distance on the up moves than on the down moves, isn't it easier to take a part out of the up move? Let's take a look at a typical uptrending chart, (Figure 5-20).

This is an example of a nice uptrend. Once the uptrend is under way, notice the size of the move up, which is shown as the distance from A to C in both cases shown on the chart. Compare this to the size of the move down, which is the distance from C to B. Notice that the move up is about twice the move down. This is not an accident. Remember, in a nice uptrend, we like to see pullbacks end in the area of a 50 percent retracement.

So, the odds are twice as good to catch a move up, since the range of motion is twice as large on a move up, correct? Actually, there are even more reasons to favor the trend. Think about it. If you are using a smaller target, your reward to risk ratio will also be smaller. This is due to the fact that the 'stop' cannot be decreased. Let's say you wanted to short the red

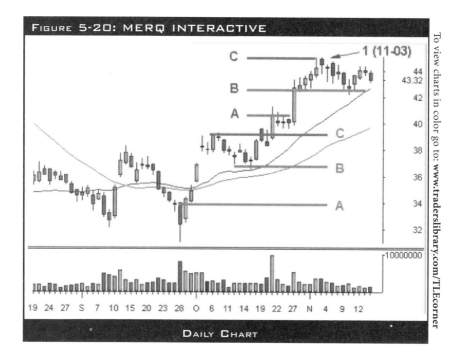

FIGURE 5-20: MERQ INTERACTIVE

DAILY CHART

bar at the arrow labeled 1. Your target is going to be half or less of the move up, yet you must still use the high of that daily bar if you are using the daily chart. So, you have a low odds play, with the reward-to-risk ratio only half of what it is on the long side. Convinced yet?

Well, what if you say that you will change the stop based on intraday charts so you can get a better risk reward? Well, here is the other catch. When playing with the trend, long in this case, the moves are usually fluid and true. When playing against the trend, short in this case, the moves are often very whippy. Look at the charts below and see what happens when you try to keep a tight stop on the play.

Let's say you try to keep your stop tighter. Next is the 5-minute chart for 11/03 (Figure 5-21), which is that first red bar on the daily chart. The stock falls hard on the initial move to point A. A logical spot to place your stop later if working on the 5-minute chart is at the point B. Notice, this gets stopped out when the stock rallies to C. Even though the

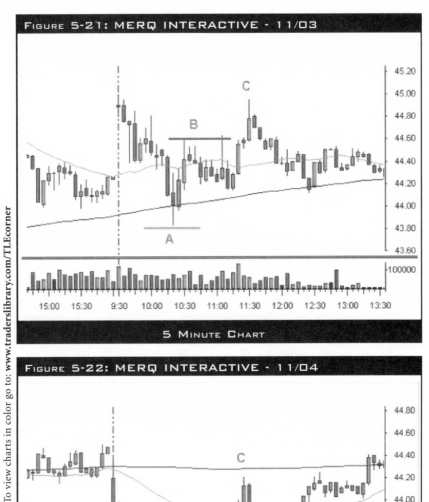

FIGURE 5-21: MERQ INTERACTIVE - 11/03

5 MINUTE CHART

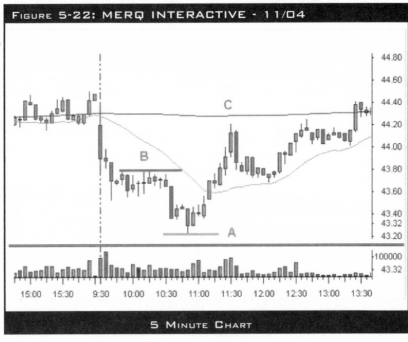

FIGURE 5-22: MERQ INTERACTIVE - 11/04

5 MINUTE CHART

daily continued down, it was hard to manage if you did not use the wide daily stop.

Try the next day, November 4 (Figure 5-22), if you saw the red bar on the daily chart the night before. Again, the stock falls hard to point A, and if you want a tighter stop than the daily chart, your only real choice is the base at B. Again, the rally trades over that stop, and continues much higher. Even though the daily chart did continue down.

The bottom line is that it's against the odds to go against the trend, it has a smaller potential target and the trade is harder to manage. Good traders know that the trend is truly your friend.

How a Trend Ends

As I've said, the trend is your friend. Traders should trade with the trend the vast majority of the time unless you understand and know what to expect. The number one mistake most traders make is trying to 'guess' when the trend will end. However, all trends do end. Understanding the signs to look for is one of the keys to successful trading. It is called a 'transition', and it will help you to know: 1.) when to exit current plays that are with the trend, 2.) when to stand aside, and 3.) when the odds are with you to play the new trend.

Take a look at the daily chart of AES Corporation (Figure 5-23). There are so many concepts on this chart, it could be the subject of several lessons. Today, I want to focus on the numbers 1-9, and the end of this trend.

On the left side of the chart, AES is in a beautiful uptrend we like to call Stage 2. There are many issues to look at on this chart, but our focus here is how this trend ends. Suffice it to say, we have higher highs and lows, and are above rising moving averages. One thing to note is that this is a very strong uptrend. The uptrend line (UTL) is very steep and the price is staying above the rising 20 period moving average (r20ma) even on pullbacks.

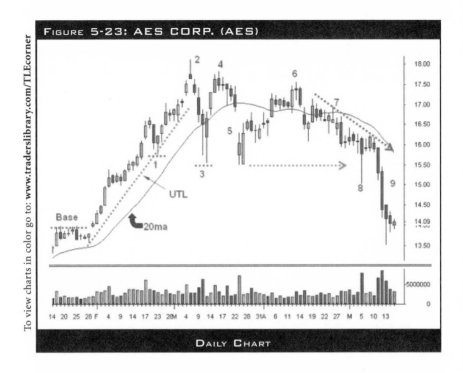

FIGURE 5-23: AES CORP. (AES)

DAILY CHART

After a long strong rally, a topping tail forms at 2. The issue to look at as the stock starts pulling back is how far and fast it pulls back. Notice the pullback to 3. Note the size of the red bars. They are the biggest on the chart at that time. Notice the bottom tails fail every day. Notice that it does not hold until it trades under the prior low pivot 1. This fall breaks the uptrend line, but that is not hard to do. Steep rallies like this create steep uptrend lines, which can break without meaning much. Note after the UTL breaks, then the last pivot also does not hold. That lower low technically 'breaks' the uptrend.

So where does the stock go from here at point 3? There is a simple concept from here. The bounce can be played long, but we do not expect to make new highs. We look for a retracement target long, (partial move to prior high) or just stand aside. Point 4 is what is key. It is a retest and failure (to break to a new high) forming a lower low pivot. Aggressive traders can short this as the top of a newly forming base, or as the beginning of a new downtrend.

Note the clear confirmation at point 5. After a four bar pullback, instead of threatening a rally, the stock gaps down. This stock has been strong prior to this and also had a four-day move down. Add to that the fact that it gapped right to the support of the last pivot 3, the gap brings in buying. However, again, the rally makes another lower high 6. As the stock broke out to 6, it came out of a small base, giving a very bullish look to the move up. However, the big picture of this stock has changed. Rallies are being used for big sellers to unload stock, and the failure of that green bar leading up to 6 is another sign of the stocks new trend.

That last sign of weakness brings in a steady pattern of selling. We are now continuing the downtrend that has already shown two or three entries. Now the stock just 'bleeds' for two weeks. Notice there is almost no buying. As the stock breaks below the major support area of pivots 3 and 6, a bottoming tail forms. The stock was quite over sold at that point, and it is not a good time to initiate new shorts. Watch the rally, and look to short the rally if the set-up is good. The rally was weak, and the next breakdown produces bearish wide range bars at point 9. Notice the bearish wide bars come after a long fall already occurred, and on big volume. This will likely end the move down for now. Notice also that we are right back to the base that started the break out.

Traders had several entries both long and short. Investors, even with a perfect entry (and I wouldn't assume that) are back to break even at best. Charts are the footprints of big money. Charts are the only thing in the market that does not lie. Learn to understand charts, and you'll learn how a trend ends.

The Intraday Trend

Many trader's like to play the intraday time frame for scalps or short day trades. Often these traders get very involved with 1, 2, and 5-minute charts, and rarely look to anything bigger. This can be a mistake, as many decisions must be made in light of the bigger time frame. They may not look to the bigger time frame, because the daily chart is too slow to show trends, or is often trendless. What is the answer? Look to a larger intraday time frame such as a 30, 60, or 180-minute chart to gain insights on your intraday bias.

Below is a 180-minute chart (Figure 5-24) of the tracking stock for the NASDAQ 100, the QQQQ. The chart pictured covers about 14 days of trading.

Coming into the left side of the chart, on May 20, we are in an uptrend. We are above a rising 20-period simple moving average, and making "higher highs" and "higher lows." When we talk about making "higher

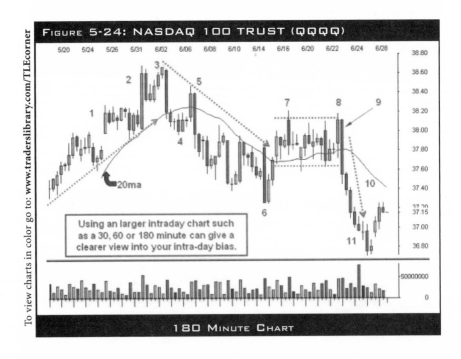

lows" we are referring to the "pivots" that form, the "V" bottoms. They are the bars that set a low, and then have a certain number of bars with higher lows on each side. When we talk about "higher highs" we are referring to the "pivots" that form, the "V" tops. They are the bars that set a high, and then have a certain number of bars with lower highs on each side.

The purpose of analyzing the trend of a chart like this is to give us a bias to the direction of the intraday chart. When this chart is in an uptrend, intraday traders should favor going long on pullbacks. Bases should be favored to break to the upside if all else is equal. When this chart stops the uptrend, it must be analyzed to see if it is going to go sideways, switch to a downtrend, or resume its former uptrend. The reverse is true for a downtrend. The best plays come while this chart is in a pure trend (either up or down).

Another good rule to follow on a chart like this is to stop playing the current trend when the price gets extended far from the 20 period moving average. This is a visual concept, but you might look at a minimum guideline of about 2 percent of the stock price.

On the chart above, the 1 represents the heart of the uptrend that is in place. The wide green bar at 2 shows the uptrend is still in place, but note that the next pivot high, 3, is barely a higher high. We are still in an uptrend, but it is a warning. Notice the next pullback, 4, makes an equal low, not a higher low. The uptrend has weakened, and when 5 puts in a lower pivot high, we can now begin playing this as a downtrend. A series of lower highs and lower lows follows and continues a nice downtrend all the way to 6.

Notice the rally off of 6 continues up strong until it trades over the prior pivot highs, a sign that the downtrend is over. The next pullback sets up a base, with a series of bars with similar highs and lows, between 7 and 8. This is congestion, confusion, and time to go easy on the intraday trades as there is no clear trend. Note the wide range red bar, 9. This is igniting a new move down and we can assume a downtrend will resume. This downtrend results in a "parabolic" drop, and by the time we approach 11, we are quite extended from the 20 period moving average. This shows it is now time to cover and relax.

Does it look easy now? Sure it does, we have the advantage of hindsight. This chart was not hand chosen; it is simply the chart of the market over the last 14 days. This works on any set of days you wish to look at. If you do not have a system for forming a market bias for your day trades, consider incorporating the intraday trend.

Finding an Intraday Reversal

The hourly chart (or anything from a 30-minute to a 180-minute chart) is an amazing chart. As a swing trader, many entries can be taken from this chart. By zooming down to the hourly chart, you can find support and resistance areas for refined entries and targets which can be used to increase probabilities and to improve the reward-to-risk on a play. Also, in tight or basing markets, the hourly chart can be used directly to swing trade. This will develop tighter stops and use smaller targets. That is exactly what is needed in a narrow market.

What about for the intraday trader? As mentioned above, the hourly can provide entry signals that can be used for day trades. Also, the 60-minute chart is key to helping us determine the intraday trend.

Additionally, it can help you find reversal points. By using the hourly chart as a guide, and then zooming down to a smaller time frame, you can find low risk entries to catch reversals intraday. The next chart is an hourly chart of the QQQQ (NASDAQ 100 Trust, tracking stock). It shows the 'NASDAQ Market' over an 11-day period. We are focusing on the last two days, 8/10 and 8/11 (Figure 5-25).

This was a choppy period in the market, in the beginning of the summer doldrums. One fact that we know at this time, there was a high degree of failure in breakouts and breakdowns. Look at the move from 1 to 2.

FIGURE 5-25: NASDAQ 100 TRUST (QQQQ)

60 MINUTE CHART

It was a parabolic drop that actually broke the support to the left. However, this happened after a six bar drop. This is not the time to short. It is better to wait for the next rally. Also, that rally may provide a tradable bounce to play long. We want to examine how to zoom down, to play this climactic move down for a bounce long. Naturally we could look for a buy set-up on the hourly chart. The problem is that the last bar is a wide bar, which will require a wide stop. Since the target is a 'retracement target', small, we cannot afford a wide stop. So let's look for a strategy on a smaller time frame.

Next we have the five minute chart of the two days in question (Figure 5-26). Let's run through the numbers posted on this chart and analyze how this pattern works.

Note at point 1, we have climactic volume setting in, as a strong move down finally makes some bottoming tails. Point 2 is a lower pivot high in

FIGURE 5-26: NASDAQ 100 TRUST (QQQQ)

5 MINUTE CHART

a downtrend. This is the first time we would not short, because the prior low is a climactic one. Point 3 is the first higher low. You don't know this as it forms, but this would be the first actionable area. As a Pristine Buy Set-up (PBS) forms and completes, it sets a higher low after a climactic bottom. While it is aggressive but the PBS here is the aggressive entry. Point 4 makes a higher high (based on pivots). Point 5 is now the first buyable PBS in a new 5-minute uptrend.

The two red lines indicate the first area of resistance. There is a void to this area, the move down was clean and smooth. That is why it rallies sharply. Point 7 is the first pullback. Is this still buyable? No. First, we just identified a resistance area that was only attacked one time. Second, remember the hourly chart? This is a rally back after a break down that we are looking for only a technical bounce. We got it.

Point 8 is a lower high, and if aggressive, could be shorted just as 3 could have been bought. If not the breakdown under point 7, or the next sell set-up could be used.

This is a common pattern we use to find an intraday change of trend. To find out more about in changes in trends, see the next two lessons.

A Change in Trend, Part 1

One of the most common mistakes for traders to make, both new and old alike, is trying to short a strong stock just because it is strong. It 'has to' turn around soon…. Like wise, some will try to buy a weak stock just because is weak. It can't go any lower… This lesson will help you look for signs of when the strong rally or fall may be ending.

I will be using the example of a strong rising stock, and when to tell weakness has set in. While this is the example, keep in mind that every-thing applies equally to the reversed situation, with a weak falling stock. Take a look at the example below. Note that this concept applies to many charts, potentially some setting up right now.

On the daily chart of HGMCY (Figure 5-27), the blue line is the 40-day moving average. The red line is the 20-day moving average. The straight green line is a trend line that was drawn in manually. This stock has been in what we call a strong Stage 2 uptrend on the daily chart from March until the beginning of June. This is evidenced by the fact that the 20 MA is rising, the 40 MA is rising, and we have the 20 above the 40 in parallel fashion. We have a clear series of higher highs and higher lows.

Notice that on all pullbacks, the 20-day moving average has worked as support. All pullbacks to this area were buyable. Any shorting attempts during this rally are low odds and have small targets. When you fight the trend, you are always fighting for a piece of the small move rather than the big move in the directions of the bigger trend.

FIGURE 5-27: HARMONY GOLD MINING CO LTD

The green trend line is drawn in for a reason. When this uptrend line is broken, it puts us on notice. Note that the uptrend is not 'broken' just because this line is broken. We are on notice to watch the new highs and lows. Notice a few clues on this chart in the area marked with 1. First, notice the large red bars, or distribution bars, are large selling. Notice the heavy volume. This is the first area that breaks the downtrend, and also breaks the 20 MA, which has held every prior time. These are clues. The break of the trend line was questionable. That is not an issue, because we are not acting here, just watching.

We are now watching for a lower high. We get it at point 2. After that, an aggressive trader can look to short the sell set-up that occurs on the daily chart at 2, or to use the next rally to short on a daily sell set-up (less aggressive).

For more strategies concerning changes in trends, read on.

A Change in Trend, Part 2

In the last lesson, I reviewed how to help identify a change in trend from a strong uptrend to a base, or possibly a downtrend. We tried to find ways to avoid the common mistake of 'shorting a strong stock' just because it has rallied too much. I now will attack the other side, which is the most common problem of all; trying to 'catch the falling knife'. In my view, the number one problem for traders is buying a stock because it can't go any lower. While we can never be sure when lows are reached, you can follow a strategy that keeps you safe and puts the odds in your favor.

This concept works on any time frame. To show this, in the previous lesson, we used a daily chart in a strong uptrend. I am now using a weak stock on a 5-minute chart for a scalp long. This is technically known as identifying the transition from Stage 4 to Stage 1.

Next is a chart of AAPL, Apple Computer, a 5-minute intraday chart (Figure 5-28). The red moving average is the 20 period and the blue is the 40 period. The pink angled line is the downtrend line drawn in, and the pink horizontal line shows the base that formed after the drop.

AAPL began a downtrend on the 5-minute chart just after noon. At 1:00 it began a sharp decline. It is a sharp decline for the following reasons: 1) Multiple large red bars. 2) The rallies are often just pauses, rather than actual rallies. 3) The downtrend line is very steep; that is, the angle of decent is large, greater than 45 degrees. 4) There are several bars down for everyone up, and little or no tails on the way down. There is little indecision here.

During a down-trend like this, the rallies are shortable. At some point, you look for clues that the fall may be ending. This would be the time to stop shorting rallies. When more evidence is present, it can be time to take aggressive longs. The first clue you look for is large volume after a multiple bar fall. We get that at 2:20. Notice that on this bar we also develop large top and bottom tails. Indecision is setting in and the volume

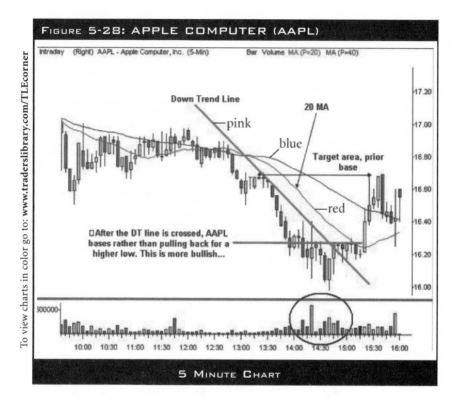

FIGURE 5-28: APPLE COMPUTER (AAPL)

Intraday (Right) AAPL - Apple Computer, Inc. (5-Min)   Bar Volume MA (P=20) MA (P=40)

Down Trend Line

20 MA

—pink

blue

Target area, prior base

—red

□After the DT line is crossed, AAPL bases rather than pulling back for a higher low. This is more bullish...

17.20
17.00
16.80
16.60
16.40
16.20
16.00

500000

10:00 10:30 11:00 11:30 12:00 12:30 13:00 13:30 14:00 14:30 15:00 15:30 16:00

5 MINUTE CHART

To view charts in color go to: www.traderslibrary.com/TLEcorner

shows that the sellers from higher prices are getting washed out. This is a good time to cover shorts and to stop shorting rallies.

We now look for a pattern to develop that indicates a trend reversal is at hand. The first thing to watch for is a break of the downtrend line, after the large volume has set in. We get that as the pink downtrend line is crossed at 2:45. This is just a 'heads up' to look for more information. We now look for a higher low to be put in. An aggressive trader would buy the higher low on a set-up on the 5-minute chart. The alternative is to wait for the rally high (at 2:45) to be broken. In this case, we get a more bullish scenario. Rather than pulling back for a higher low, the stock bases sideways, a sign of even greater strength. The play is now to buy the stock over this base that has just formed. For a play like this, the target is a retracement target. We look for less than a 50% retracement of the fall that occurred, or to the first area of minor resistance, such as a base that was previously support.

Remember, to be successful in trading, always look out for the changes in trends

Trading Gaps, Part 1

Gaps are a category all unto themselves. I will discuss gaps in two parts. We will look at what they are, why they happen and what the concepts are. In the next lesson, we will look at some chart examples.

A gap is a term used to describe the condition when a stock opens at a significantly higher or lower price than it closed the prior day. It refers to the gap that is left in the daily chart. It is the empty space from yesterday's close to today's open. However, gaps can also gap into the prior days trading range, making it less obvious on a daily chart. Gaps can be either up or down. They can happen to all stocks, listed or NASDAQ.

The gap is measured from the prior day's 4:00 PM closing price to the current day's 9:30 AM opening price. All times are Eastern Standard Time. The post market activity and pre-market activity do not affect the gap for our purposes. Stocks can trade after market hours through ECNs (Electronic Communication Networks) until 8:00 PM and pre-market starting at 8:00 AM, but this is currently not considered normal market hours. Many stocks may gap a small amount every day, but our focus on gapping stocks is on those that are gapping significantly.

For example, stock XYZ closes at 4:00 PM at 37. It trades in after market hours up to 38. The next day at 8:00 AM, it starts trading at 38.5 and trades up to 39.5. By 9:30, the stock is all the way back down to 37.10. The gap as we measure it is only 10 cents. All of the post-market and pre-market trades do not matter in looking at whether a stock is gapping, though you may want to be aware of those trades when planning a strategy. The stock traded, and people made and lost money, but the gap is not affected (Figure 5-29).

What causes gaps? Usually it is news driven. Individual stocks can gap up or down due to news such as earnings reports, earnings pre-announcements, analyst's upgrades and downgrades, rumors, message board posts, CNBC, key people in the company commenting or buying/selling the company stock.

Groups of stocks or the whole market may gap up or down due to various economic reports, news on the economy, political news, or major world events (like the large gap down from the 9-11 incident). This news can cause many individual issues to gap with the market. Many big name stocks move very closely with the market. Some may be in the sectors that are most affected by the news.

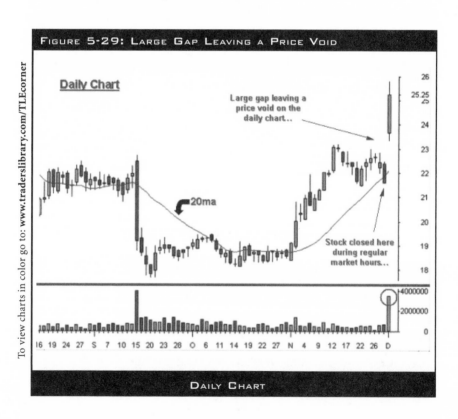

FIGURE 5-29: LARGE GAP LEAVING A PRICE VOID

Whatever the exact reason, gaps are the result of some kind of event happening while the market is closed. The result is either buying or selling pressure at open the next day that will make the stock open at a different price than where it closed. Why are they important? This sudden move by a stock, the sudden change in demand, is often the beginning or a major move. There are swing trading strategies that capitalize on entering after a gap, and guerrilla tactics that capitalize on one or two day moves after a gap.

Some concepts and general rules about gaps. First, we generally never buy a large gap up at the open. Generally, we never sell short a large gap down at the open. When Market makers have the chance, they will often exaggerate the gap. Also, large gaps are already extended, making the play risky. We tend to fade the gap initially, if played at all. Fading means to play the stock to come back in to where it was. Fading a large gap up would be to go short the stock as it trades down after a large gap up. However, this is a general rule and we must look to the stock we will be trading.

In general, you must keep in mind that the stock is opening at a price that thousands of people have decided it should be trading at after digesting whatever news occurred. You cannot look at the news and decide the stock is overvalued or undervalued. That defies the basic concept of technical analysis. Keep your mind open to the fact, that regardless of any gap, for any reason, a stock can still move in either direction. Gaps do not have to be filled, but often are.

After the initial move, the charts must be looked at along with the amount of the gap, and the share price of the stock. The daily chart, the extension of moves, support and resistance levels, and relative strength all come into play. Small gap downs that gap under support can be watched for short entries. Large gap downs that gap above support can be watched for long entries. What is large or small and what is resistance is all a matter of chart reading and interpretation.

The concept of gaps is a very difficult one for most traders, even those with considerable experience. They are a strategy all by themselves and are part of many other strategies I teach. Study gaps all you can. Study them when they happen. Learn the strategies and get familiar with them. We will look at a few examples in the next lesson. While this cannot serve to fully educate you on the topic, it can get you started thinking correctly about a big part of the trading day, the opening.

Trading Gaps, Part 2

In the last lesson, I started a discussion about gaps. I talked about what they are, how they form, and why they form. While there are many strategies involving gaps, let's look at a few examples here.

As a rule, we like to buy strength and sell, or sell short weakness. This is the preferred play. There are exceptions. Next is an example of a stock that had a bullish pattern and looked poised to move higher (Figure 5-30). In this case, the bullishness is what sets up the short, as traders are trapped by the large gap down.

This stock gapped below an entire bullish WRB just as it looked like it was set to break out of a consolidation. While the gap makes the stock appear extended to the downside, remember this gap is a vacuum that happened when the market was closed and traders were not trading. It was likely news-driven and those long in the stock have no opportunity to get out at a favorable price. So the selling begins even after the big gap.

Figure 5-31 is an example of a long play.

Here we have a stock that has been in a bullish uptrend. Selling begins and 3 red bars appear. Two of these we would classify as WRBs. Is this the end of the up trend? The next day the stock gaps up, almost half way into the prior WRB. If this stock can hold the prior day's low (the WRB), it is poised to move higher. The shock of the gap stops the shorts and the uptrend resumes.

FIGURE 5-30: TIVO INC. (TIVO)

DAILY CHART

FIGURE 5-31: VERISIGN INC. (VRSN)

DAILY CHART

Gaps come in all varieties and many of them become difficult to play. Many times the right combination of events comes together for a clear play. We look to the prior price pattern, the amount of the gap, the relative strength of the gap compared to the broader market and support and resistance, among other things. Some of the best combinations are given names as regular strategies. You should look to this list of possible combinations to find gaps that are tradable when the bigger picture is not as clear.

There are some nice things about playing gaps that many traders like. Sometimes, you can have tight stops (or can pass on the ones where you do not), and you usually get some results fairly quickly. Often, reversal time (10:00 AM) brings some results.

This is a sampling of some of the many strategies we use with gaps. This, along with the last lesson, will provide a firm foundation as you continue to expand your trading knowledge.

Chapter 6
Chart Lessons on the Market

The NASDAQ in Review

Most every day I am asked, "Where do you think the market is going tomorrow?" It is the most common question that all traders want to ask. Well, the answer is always something like, "It is definitely going up, unless it heads down!"

While the answer always gets a laugh, I do go on to give my best interpretation of the current direction. However the truth is that no one knows where the market will be tomorrow, in a week, in a month, or in a year. The further away, the less likely one is to know market direction. For example, I may be able to give some insight into where the market may be tomorrow much better than I can predict where we may be in a year. With political events, economic issues, interest rates, companies giving earnings warnings, upgrades and downgrades, it becomes impossible to predict the future. One of the reasons I like to trade is because trading is not dependent on the question, "Where is the market going?" Traders look for opportunities each day, regardless of direction, and are willing to change course in a minute, if needed.

There is much to be gained by having a good understanding of likely possibilities of where the market may be heading, based on the charts. I will always try to develop scenarios of what may happen over the next few days. This is all that is really relevant if you day and swing trade. This understanding can be very useful, while not fool proof.

Look at the chart below. It is the NASDAQ Composite Index from some April lows (Figure 6-1). There is a 20 MA (red) and a 50 MA (blue).

April was the month the NASDAQ rallied hard, and has been in a trading range ever since. This range was playable. Would you have been able to navigate through the last three months? The following charts are all the same exact chart of the NASDAQ, with various points and trend lines added along the way.

In figure 6-2, I have added letters A and B at two consolidation areas. Letters C to G and numbers 1 to 6 represent key high and low points.

Look at consolidation area A. It started with a large green bar on 4/5 that came after a large gap opened right off the recent low. At the time, we discussed that this was to be watched, but at the time it was no more than a small rally in the middle of a downtrend. However, the 3-day consolidation and subsequent gap up on April 10 started to get our attention.

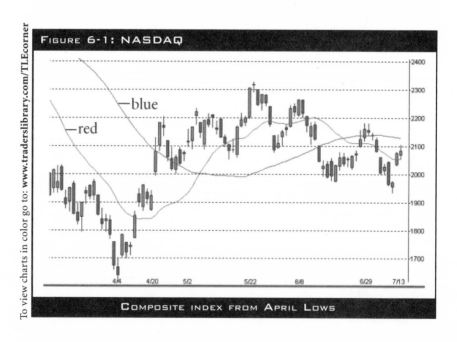

FIGURE 6-1: NASDAQ

COMPOSITE INDEX FROM APRIL LOWS

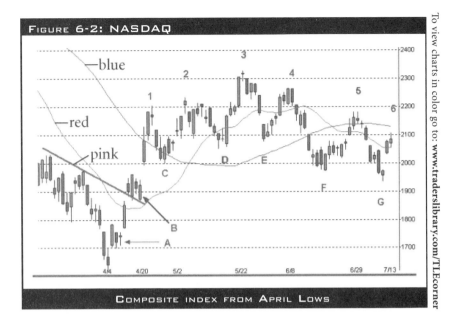

To view charts in color go to: www.traderslibrary.com/TLEcorner

Notice the gap up the next day, (first bar in the 4-day consolidation at B) did sell off but only a small amount. Normally, a gap up after the previous day's up that sold off would sell off in a big way. Instead it held its gains.

Notice also that this gap to consolidation B took it above its downtrend line, which is drawn in pink. While this 4 day consolidation went on, the market did not make any attempt to pull back. It was during this time that we looked to be bullish for a bounce.

You see that the bounce came as the market rallied up to point 1 as shown on the next chart (Figure 6-3).

Anyone remaining bullish during this 4-day consolidation was rewarded nicely, as the gap up led to a 3-day rally that ended with a Doji day at the high at 1. Notice, three days up, Doji day, and a gap down the next day means it is time for the profit taking sell off. What is a likely target? Three days down to the low of the last gap up day. That pullback takes you right to point C. Notice how as we form points 2 and D, that all moves are going in 3-7 gap moves up or down and are going right to the

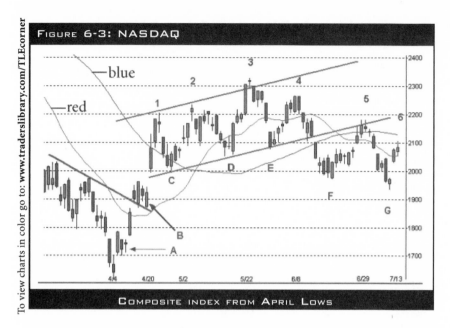

FIGURE 6-3: NASDAQ

COMPOSITE INDEX FROM APRIL LOWS

established trend lines. We recognized being range bound at this point. We were playing the market to turn after hitting one of these trend lines after 3-7 days in one direction. Notice point 3 broke the trend line by a little. The Doji the next day gave you your warning and the trade down the next day was the confirmation that the break of the uptrend line was just a 'technical' one. This actually then became the head of the head and shoulders pattern formed with 2 and 4 and the shoulders and 3 as the head.

Now draw your attention to point 4. This was a very important point. Point 4 stopped short of the top of the uptrend line. This is critical. We went very bearish when the market traded down on that red bar day, just after the big green bar which makes the top at point 4. Failing to reach the top of the channel, means that there is a chance that the next trip down may break below the channel.

Now, draw your attention to the final chart below (Figure 6-4).

While 4 failed to make a higher high, F went on to make a lower low. This is an indication of a change in trend. This makes point 3 the inflection or pivot point. We now start a series of lower lows and lower highs. Notice again, the high points which are numbers 3 through 6 and the lows, letters E through G, form very nice trend lines and all have three to seven bars up or down (with one exception).

At the time, we are showing signs of not making it to the top of the trend line. If this becomes true, be careful of the next low H, as it will be in question to hold.

The bottom line is to be flexible, find opportunities, and try to prepare for the turning points that the charts provide.

A Look at the Market

Let's take time out to analyze the market, looking at where we have been, and what we can use for a strategy for going forward. While we cannot predict future events, we can use the odds that the chart patterns give us to form strategies that can be played.

As a personal preference, I am going to look at the NASDAQ. The chart below is the QQQ, the NASDAQ 100 tracking stock (Figure 6-5). A good analysis should involve the broader market and key sectors as well.

During most of 2003, the QQQ was in a Stage 2 uptrend. Among other things, you might recognize the smooth rising 20-period moving average (20MA), as well as an uptrend line (UT Line), that are both respected by the price on pullbacks. The price pattern shows continuous higher highs and higher lows. During this time period, pullbacks are buyable using the proper strategies.

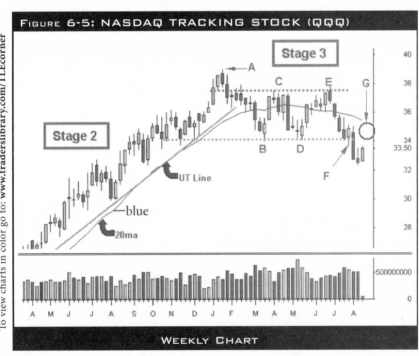

To view charts in color go to: www.traderslibrary.com/TLEcorner

At the point labeled A, we have just set new highs on a powerful move. Halfway in between A and B, when we stall at the 20MA, we are still in Stage 2. After stalling for a few bars, we break below the 20MA and the UT line. This gives us a 'heads up' to be cautious, but we are still in Stage 2.

At the point when we reach B, we have a buy set-form. It is playable as a long but we no longer expect a new high on the next rally. Why? First, the trend line break, and second, the fact that the last pullback came all the way down to major support (the green line at point B). We do not know this for sure, but the chart is telling us that, odds are, it is unlikely to move to new highs in the same fluid manner as we have in the past year. As we roll over at point C, we now have an official 'equal low' and 'lower high', and the uptrend is now officially over. This now looks like it has completed a transition to a base. At this point we cannot tell if it is a bullish base that is just resting before a new move up, or a bearish base that may signal an upcoming Stage 4. Points D and E make a perfect confirmation of the base, and the sideways trend continues.

As soon as you recognize that the uptrend is over, it is time to adjust strategies. Swing trades from the daily will be different, and it is time to move up stops on long-term bullish positions. New strategies are introduced that play the base until it breaks.

Point F starts off like just another pullback to the major support of the base. The green bar was a bounce that appeared quite playable on the daily charts (this is a weekly). It was not wrong to play this as a long, at least on the daily charts. However, the market often speaks loudest when it speaks in failures. Here is the time where the base does not hold. It is near August 1, and this base was playable all year long. Now the failure to hold this base means a break down and likely transition into Stage 4, the downtrend.

How do you handle the move? The odds-on strategy is to short the rally that comes back to the base, as identified by the circle at G. Now under-

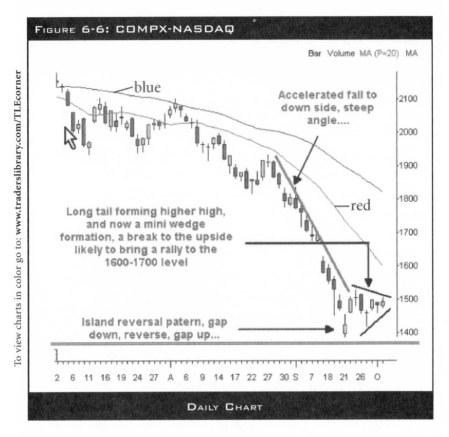

FIGURE 6-6: COMPX-NASDAQ

Bar Volume MA (P=20) MA

blue

Accelerated fall to down side, steep angle....

red

Long tail forming higher high, and now a mini wedge formation, a break to the upside likely to bring a rally to the 1600-1700 level

Island reversal patern, gap down, reverse, gap up...

DAILY CHART

To view charts in color go to: www.traderslibrary.com/TLEcorner

stand that it requires a strategy and set-up to short—you do not do it blindly at a certain price point. If this sets up properly but fails to follow through to the down side, this failure and the bullishness to stop-out that set-up will likely be an indication to be long. Again, a failure of a good pattern speaks the loudest.

If you want to follow the forward-looking analysis of this lessons, be sure to understand the strategies involved, and the fact that we play odds. When the odds don't play out, we use protective stops.

A NASDAQ Update, Part 1

I would like to take another lesson to review some basic charting, how we apply it to the market, and how you can and cannot benefit from it.

The chart I will be reviewing is the daily chart of the NASDAQ (Figure 6-6). The lower line is the 20 period moving average, the upper is the 50 period moving average.

There was a steep decline that happened over the prior month. This steep fall was after a long move down by the NASDAQ. The gap down, green bar, and then gap up is what is known as an island reversal. It is often a bottom formation after a prior move to the downside. Note that after the island reversal, the next seven days are rather tight and do not challenge the low area. The one day that came close developed a long tail, showing that the buyers were now strong in this area. It was stated that a move above that wedge would likely rally to fill the gap in the chart in the 1700 level.

Here is another chart of the NASDAQ (Figure 6-7). Let's review what has happened and how it was played. Point A is the green bar that happened the day after the last chart was posted.

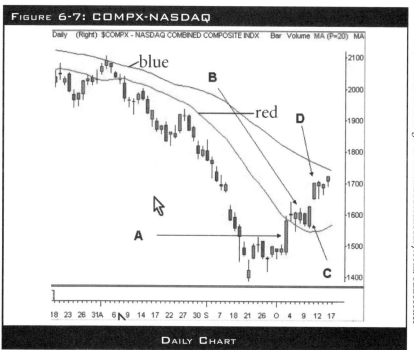

Figure 6-7: COMPX-NASDAQ

Daily (Right) $COMPX - NASDAQ COMBINED COMPOSITE INDX   Bar Volume MA (P=20) MA

blue

B

red   D

A

C

18 23 26 31A 6 9 14 17 22 27 30 S 7 18 21 26 O 4 9 12 17

DAILY CHART

To view charts in color go to: www.traderslibrary.com/TLEcorner

Now, let's talk about how to play this. It is difficult to play the first day up when this starts. If you are prepared and aggressive, entering longs over 30 minute highs is a good strategy. We already had DELL and on this day we added YHOO at 10.15. The issue now becomes; will these gains hold or will selling step in as it has in the past? So, we monitor the next day's point B. The more that chart pulls back in price, the weaker the market is and the less likely to be able to keep gains and continue the move up. If the market pulls back more than 50 percent of that move up, it is suspect. Notice the market moved sideways. It corrected through time, not through price. This is the most bullish scenario. The sellers never outnumbered the buyers, even after the move up. So we prepare for another move up.

Focus on point C, the large green bar at the end of the 5-day base. This bar is known as a "bullish engulfing bar." It opens below the prior day's low, and closes above the prior day's high. It almost does this for the entire 5-day base.

Now, area D starts the process over again. Mark off the high of bar D and the low of bar C. Monitor the percent of pullback to gauge the selling pressure and strength. This move takes us to the original target, filling the gap to the 1700 area. As of this moment, the set up looks bullish again. A gap up or move up again into the 50 period moving average would be a good time to sell swing positions that were acquired during this time. Cores are an individual situation that could range from long term holds, to selling part positions, to taking protective measures such as selling calls or buying puts to hedge.

Nothing is certain in charting or technical analysis. There is no magic indicator or moving average. It is just a matter of combining several tools with common sense to try to get the odds in your favor. Then, use good money management, and have a lot of patience and discipline.

A NASDAQ Update, Part 2

The NASDAQ composite has set up an interesting scenario over the last week. The charts that follow are of the QQQ, which is the NASDAQ 100 Ttrust, commonly used to trade the NASDAQ 100 and mirrors its pattern. There are several issues that will be discussed in this lesson, including trend analysis, multiple time frame resolution, low volume holiday moves, head and shoulders patterns, and pattern failure.

Below is a weekly chart of the QQQ (Figure 6-8). It is always best to start with the larger time frame and work your way down. The weekly QQQ had been in a downtrend for over two years. As of October, it set a new low, which was just another in a long series of new lows (marked L1). The rally that ensued in October and November was different because it rallied above a prior major pivot high (H1). This puts the weekly downtrend in question and requires a close to see if the next pullback puts in a higher low (marked '?').

To take a closer look at this pullback on the weekly, we zoom in by looking at the daily chart (Figure 6-9) to see how this pullback on the weekly looks on the daily, to get clues as to where a possible entry may be found.

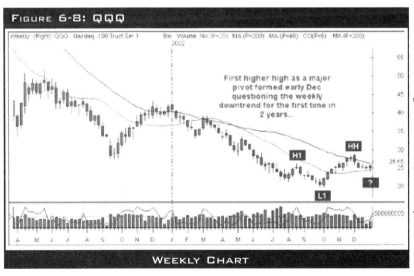

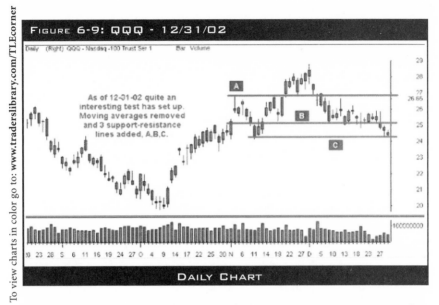

FIGURE 6-9: QQQ - 12/31/02

DAILY CHART

Above is a daily chart of the QQQ with the moving averages removed to focus on the price bars. Support and resistance lines have been added. Line A is the high from the beginning of November, and an area that the market should have held during the December pullback if a strong uptrend were going to stay in place. Line B is the bottom of the base that formed in December, and the minor support formed by the base from late October. Line C is the support area from the last major pivot from before the December base. Notice that the high of the base on the December 12 spikes up to Line A, at the prior high formed at the beginning of November. This has formed what many labeled a potential 'head and shoulders' formation over the months of November and December. Note also that the 'right shoulder' has a lengthy base. Trading below this base would be considered very bearish and may even be considered anticipatorily 'breaking' the neckline of the head and shoulders pattern. Most would not really consider the neckline broken until Line C was violated.

However, regardless of any head and shoulders formation, the fact that the market traded below the December base is bearish. A base like that sets up an area of supply that should be difficult to trade through. So, is

FIGURE 6-10: QQQ - 1/6/03

DAILY CHART

this a bearish outlook at this point? Well, one more consideration, this base formed mostly under extremely light holiday volume. This makes the base much weaker, as fewer hands have participated in the base. The ability to break through the base on light volume is greater than a base with heavy volume. So, the plan at this point for long term trades would be to short a rally attempt that falls somewhere under the base, and enter short swing positions when a prior day's low has been violated. Naturally, every day provides intraday possibilities for day trades, but longer-term trades must be initiated at likely turning points. Therefore, the need for a plan from the daily charts becomes even more important.

Above is the same daily NASDAQ chart, with the next three trading days added (Figure 6-10). The support-resistance lines have been removed and simple moving averages added back on. Note that the first new day was a very powerful green candle. We have already entered the base on this one trading day. Moves like this can be powerful, and the volume returned to a more normal area on this advance. Over the next two days, we have advanced to the top of the December base. The plan of shorting never comes into play, as the move goes right through the resistance of the base without hesitation. This changes the odds of what is likely to happen in the future. This rally is likely to stall here. It is a 3-4 day advance, and has run into the 200 day moving average. While this moving average is not actual price resistance, it is a well-known landmark among traders. This is likely to cause a pause in this area, along with the fact that there is still some resistance that may be left from the top of the base.

The current plan is to monitor this upcoming pullback. If it is mild, and stays in the upper part of the 4-day advance, or simply bases sideways, the odds will favor long term positions and the completion of the weekly Pristine Buy Set-up (see Appendix A) in a bullish way. Now that the weekly Pristine Buy Set-up has hit, we will look to the daily charts for an entry possibility for swing and core positions. There may be added fuel to the rally, as many may have considered this a complete head and shoulders pattern, and this rally may have caught several shorts off guard. Trading under the lows of the last two weeks would likely bring about weakness that would lead to a test of the NASDAQ lows.

Analysis of the NASDAQ charts can provide background knowledge for future trades and, ultimately, trading success.

The Volatility Index as a Guide

The Market Volatility Index (VIX, symbol VIX.X on Realtick) is provided by the Chicago Board of Options Exchange (CBOE) and used as a guide to indicate the level of anxiety or complacency of the market. It does this by measuring how much people are willing to pay to buy options on the S&P 100 futures (OEX).

The price of an option is made of several components. However, options do trade independently and have their own supply and demand factors just like any instrument would. All of the components of the option price (such as the price of the underlying issue and the time to expiration) can be determined except for one. That one component is the volatility, or the 'excess' amount people are willing to pay for the option.

While it does measure the volatility of both call and put options, it is primarily the put options that bring on the higher levels of volatility that are being measured. The reason for this is simple. Most people are focused on owning stocks or being long on the market. To protect portfolios, investors will buy puts to hedge against market declines. While puts could be bought on most individual stocks, it is easier and more cost efficient to buy them on the 'market' in general. Options on the S&P 100 futures are very liquid and the most common way to protect long portfolios. Also, speculators who want to participate in market declines may buy the 'OEX Puts' to profit.

How does it work? It is a type of contrarian indicator. When 'everyone' wants OEX Puts, the fear in the market is great and 'everyone' causes demand to go up. The price of the options go up which is reflected as the 'volatility' component of the price of the option. This is what is measured by the VIX. Once everyone has taken protective downside measures, the question becomes; who is left to sell stocks? This is known as a washout of sellers. Like any indicator, it cannot be used by itself to predict market action. It is an excellent tool for looking for extreme readings to help confirm other indications of a market turn.

Like any chart, we can look at the VIX to determine trend, support and resistance levels, and relationship to moving averages, on all time frames. The most practical use is to help confirm longer-term turning points in the market. Look at the next chart (Figure 6-11).

As a reference, the VIX peaked out at 57.3 during the September 11, 2001 crisis period. Note that it was not until late July 2002 that we revisited that area. This was the first time the NASDAQ made any attempt to hold from the decline of 2002. The VIX was an excellent guide to watch during 2002, as the fall in the NASDAQ, even when it challenged the September 2001 lows, did not bring about a confirming rise in the VIX.

In October 2002, when the NASDAQ put in its bottom, it was well anticipated by the VIX, as the VIX hit resistance from its previous high.

FIGURE 6-11: VIX (TOP); NAS (BOTTOM)

At this point, for the VIX to go any higher would have been challenging the October 2001 crisis levels. There was a great deal of 'anxiety' in the NASDAQ at this time. The predictive value it had in late November 2002, actually turned and started heading up well before the NASDAQ headed down.

While no tool can predict market action, the VIX does an excellent job measuring the useful components of anxiety and complacency. Use it as a guide to help you confirm possible turning points in the market.

Caution in the Market

Trading is all about playing the probabilities. It is looking at a stock through multiple time frames and determining if there are odds that the stock is more likely to move in one direction or another. It is also about finding these areas, or focal points and reacting to them properly, whether the expected outcome plays out or if the unexpected happens.

Right now there are several things coming together in the broader market that give us reason to use caution. When I say the broader market, I am referring to the S&P 500. It can be viewed as the SPY (the S&P Depository Receipts) or the S&P Futures. We at times may look at the NASDAQ separately. These two will often mirror each other; sometimes, they will deviate.

First, let's take a look at the bigger picture. We have experienced a strong uptrend in the daily and weekly market charts, and we have advocated buying all pullbacks during this stage. This is what is done until the charts give us clues that momentum may be ending. The fact that momentum may be ending is what we want to look at.

Look at the daily chart of the SPY (Figure 6-12).

We have a nice uptrend, as identified by a long series of higher highs and higher lows. We have a rising 20 period moving average and a nicely formed trend line. The recent highest high was made in mid-June and it is labeled HH2. This first pullback after HH2 is steep, and trades under the pivot point on June 9 labeled HL1 for higher low 1. This first pullback is labeled LL1 for Lower Low 1. While this is technically a Lower Low, this is still a bullish pattern at the time LL1 forms. The pullback was steep, but so was the rally that preceded it. Also the June 9 pivot is not a potent one, as it consists of two minor pivots and occurs during a very strong move up.

The next rally after LL1 fails to make a new high. Even more bearish is the fact that it fails on two attempts. That shallow pullback between

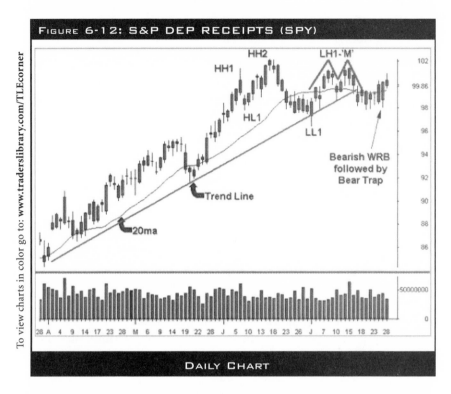

FIGURE 6-12: S&P DEP RECEIPTS (SPY)

DAILY CHART

attempts forms what is known as an M pattern. The bearishness of this pattern is obvious. The left part of the M fails to make a new high. A shallow pullback comes, getting the Bull's hopes up for the next rally to go to new highs. When the second attempt (the right side of the M) fails to trade higher than the first attempt, hopes are dashed, and selling comes in as the pattern trades below the middle of the M. This whole M forms a lower high, breaking the pattern of the uptrend.

The pullback has not made a new low (under LL1). What has occurred is likely a transition from the Bullish Stage 2 to a sideways consolidation know as Stage 3. Of course we can never be sure until after that fact; however as traders, playing the probabilities is what we do.

Use this with some other information. At the time of this writing we had an extended rally on the weekly charts without any real correction. We were entering the time known as the "summer doldrums." August is often a light volume month with little follow through in price action. August, September, and October are statistically the most bearish months, according to the *Traders Almanac*.

How do you use this information during the summer months? I would say it is a time to watch the daily charts and expect things to be range bound until we break out of this area. Expect less movement, that is, less of a target on trades. Reduce trading, and lighten up on shares. Use caution. Take that vacation you have been waiting for.

Chapter 7
Lessons on Classic Patterns

Using Relative Strength as One of Your Tools

Every day I like to have five tools, or weapons, if you will, at my disposal. First is a watch list, created from the daily charts the night before, for swing trades and the best trends for intraday trades. Second, I have the gap list from the morning, used largely for guerrilla trading tactics. Third, I have a list of favorite stocks to review, stocks that are high volume and easy to trade. Fourth, I have intraday scanning devices, such as Pristine ESP™. Fifth, I have a page set up in my Real Tick platform that shows the different indices, and a page set up for each index.

Two of these lists can be very helpful in determining a stock's *relative strength*. When a stock has relative strength, it means that the stock is acting stronger than the market in general, or stronger than the index it is in. An index can also have relative strength compared to the market. For example, on a down day in the market, the Semi Conductor index may be down the same percentage as the market as measured by either the NASDAQ or the S&P 500. The charts may also look similar. But the Retail Index may be up on the day, with a chart that shows intraday up-trend. This would then be a case of the Retail Index showing great relative strength. Perhaps Wal-Mart is up more than the rest of the Retail Index and is breaking out. It would have good relative strength compared to the

Retail Index and great relative strength compared to the S&P 500. All the same is true, in reverse, for relative weakness.

One of these lists shows stocks that are at the top 10 percent and bottom 10 percent of the day's trading range. Picture a market that is in an uptrend on daily charts, but in the middle of a pullback in the middle of the morning. The trend is up, but we are pulling back 50 percent of the days trading range to an area of support. Looking at stocks that are close to the days high (top 10 percent of the day's trading range) will give a list of stocks that have a good chance of moving up if the market holds on the pullback and continues up. Playing these stocks on appropriate set-ups would mean playing stocks that are relatively strong. Playing the ones that also have good chart set-ups would mean taking advantage of more than one strategy; this can make for a very good play. The same is true in reverse for finding relative weakness.

Next, check your Real Tick page on market indices and look for the strongest index. Look at daily and 15-minute chart patterns, and look at % gain on a watch list. Find the strong sectors and weak sectors. Then turn to a page that has a list of stocks in that sector. Look at them in a watch list and in 5-minute charts. Look for patterns that defy the current market or sector chart.

The following page shows charts of the NASDAQ futures from December 11 (Figures 7-1 and 7-2). The market was looking strong all day after a Fed announcement, but very suddenly got hit hard in the afternoon.

Notice the afternoon base, when it was taken out, and the 200 period moving average in blue.

The Semi Conductors held the afternoon base for a long time while the market dropped (Figure 7-2). Turning to a Real Tick page with all of the Semi Conductor components on it revealed many 5-minute charts that looked the same as the market; except one; SANM, shown in figure 7-3.

This chart defied the market. An example of what we call an "afternoon jammin' session." The stock was being bought. As the market finally sta-

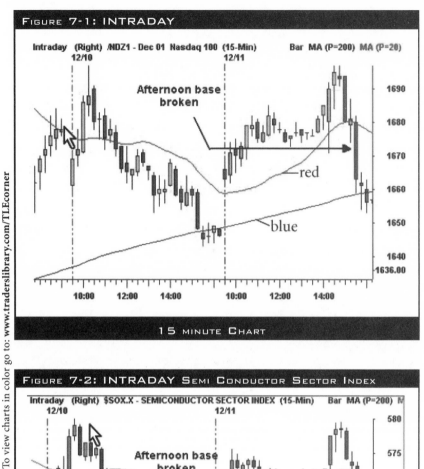

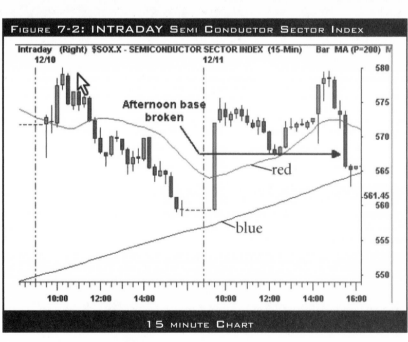

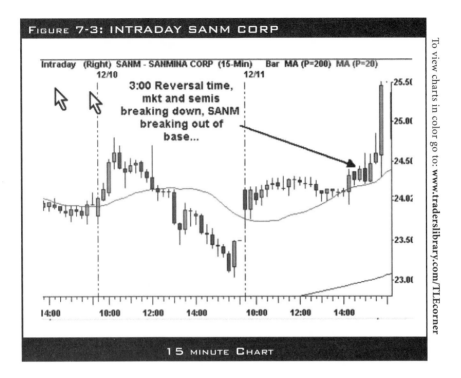

FIGURE 7-3: INTRADAY SANM CORP

Intraday (Right) SANM - SANMINA CORP (15-Min)   Bar MA (P=200) MA (P=20)

3:00 Reversal time, mkt and semis breaking down, SANM breaking out of base...

15 MINUTE CHART

bilized at the 200 period moving average on the 15-minute chart, as if often does, look what SANM did, breaking out of the base.

I have shown you two methods of using relative strength to help you in your trading. Relative strength is often strong enough to base some intraday trades on but, when combined with proper chart set-ups, it can be very powerful.

Relative Strength at Reversal Time

This lesson is about a simple tool that should be considered on all your trades. Often it is so powerful, it can be the driving reason behind a trade. It is the concept of relative strength, especially when you time the entry with a reversal time. The same concepts apply to finding relative weakness when shorting. For this lesson, I will be using the concept of relative strength.

By relative strength, I am not referring to the indicator known as RSI, but to a stock's strength or weakness at the moment when compared to the market as a whole, or the particular sector to which the stock belongs. The concept of relative strength can be used on any time frame, and is only valid in that time frame. For example, a stock showing great relative strength on a 5-minute chart is a stock which has a 5-minute chart that appears stronger than the 5-minute chart of the market. To judge the market, you could look at the NASDAQ or S&P 500, or use the futures of either of these, or the tracking symbols of SPY (for the S&P) or QQQ (for the NASDAQ 100). It would be valid to look at this for a scalp or possibly to enter a day trade, but if it does not show any relative strength on the daily chart, it would not be favored for a swing trade.

When I say that the 5-minute chart is stronger, I mean specifically that the bars making up the chart show greater strength if you were looking to go long. Perhaps the stock is making a higher high or higher low, but the market is not. Perhaps the down bars are not as long. Perhaps the stock stays in the upper half of the day's trading range while the market or sector does not. Perhaps the stock holds a support area while the similar support area in the market or sector does not hold. Perhaps the stock stays above a rising 20 period moving average, while the market is below. In extreme cases, the stock may be basing at the high of the day stays making new highs, while the market is pulling back or making a new low.

Let's look at a 5-minute chart of Genesis Corp. (GNSS) (Figure 7-4), with a chart of the SPY (Figure 7-5). The relative strength became obvious between 9:50 and 10:20 AM EST. The blue line is the 20 period moving average on both charts.

Notice the arrows labeled A and B. These point to the 4th and 8th bar on both 5-minute charts. At 9:50 the SPY was drifting lower and GNSS had three WRBs up on the 5-minute chart. The plan was to watch the pullback, since we identified a strong stock.

The end of the first reversal time (9:50-10:10) brought a new low in the SPY, and a higher low in GNSS, at Minor Support, at the rising 20 period moving average. The 5-minute Pristine Buy Set-up (see Appendix A) was played, based on this set-up. The markets were generally in uptrends at this time, though this is not evident by the 5-minute chart.

At 10:30, GNSS had tested the high of the day, which was the first target. Now the decision to hold half for bigger gains became easy, as the SPY recovered and was challenging new highs for the day (Figure 7-5). If the stock was strong without the market helping, it should do even better with the market. The back half was held into the next day. Also of note in making this decision was the daily chart. It was showing a nice 1-2-3 continuation play.

When trading you want as many factors on your side as possible. While this stock showed up with nice relative strength, it was also being watched due to the bullish daily set-up as discussed above. At the time of entry,

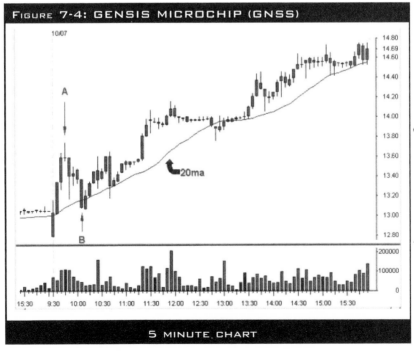

FIGURE 7-4: GENSIS MICROCHIP (GNSS)

5 MINUTE CHART

we had a 5-minute PBS, at mS, at the r20ma, with a NRB and COG and committed volume on the first move up. Relative strength (or weakness when shorting) should be one of the factors you use to help you in assessing trades.

Failed Breakdown at Reversal Time

In the previous lesson, we looked at a 'relative strength at reversal time play.' This play is on the other end of the relative strength scale. What set up this play is the weakness going into reversal time.

I am sure you noticed that both of these plays refer to reversal time. Does that give you the impression that it is an important topic? It should. Reversal times are certain times of the day that we know stocks are most likely to change their patterns. This may be from down to up, or may just be from down to sideways. A sideways base may break down or break

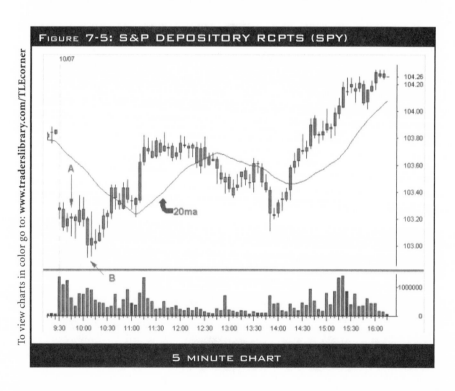

FIGURE 7-5: S&P DEPOSITORY RCPTS (SPY)

5 MINUTE CHART

out. The key times we focus on are 9:35, 9:50-10:10, 10:25-10:35, 11:00-11:15, 12:00, 1:30, 2:15-2:30, 3:00, and 3:30. Note these are all Eastern Standard Time (market opens at 9:30). Try this. Print out intraday charts of the market, or your favorite stocks. Circle the major areas on the chart. Circle the highs, lows, and major reversals. You will be amazed at how often they line up within one 5-minute bar of the above times. This is especially true for the time periods around 10:00, 10:30, and entering and leaving lunch.

Figure 7-6 is a 5-minute chart of Marvell Technology Group.

This stock bounced off the minor support area just before 10:00. Its 30-minute low was established in a strong support area. Shortly after that, the stock broke down below the support area, and under the current low of the day (after almost an hour of trading). This must be a short, right?

Actually it is a very nice long. The long was called at $44.49 with a target of $44.99. Let's look a little closer.

1. The support area the bears claim was not broken. It is a wide area, which also has support at the bottom of the base.

2. Many traders will look at the break of 30-minute lows as a bearish sign. It often is. However, how you get there makes the difference. This stock gapped up and fell for an hour straight. This should take it off of your shorting list on an intraday basis. It needs to bounce, or consolidate for a period of time before you look at shorting this.

3. What often happens is that novices short this break of 30-minute lows, only to find it is done falling. This produces a short covering rally, which may carry over to everyone who has shorted that day.

4. Last and perhaps most important, look at figure 7-7. This may scare you a bit. This is the same stock, same day, looked at through the eyes of a 15-minute chart. Using Multiple Time Frames to analyze every trade is a concept I spend a good deal of time on. Does this look like a short?

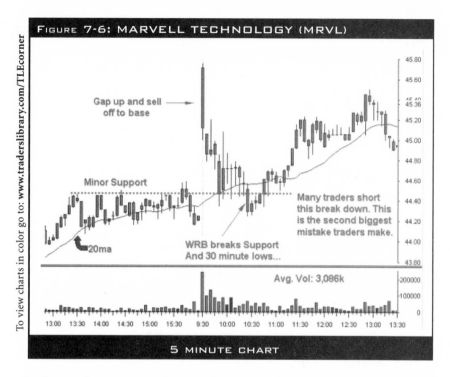

FIGURE 7-6: MARVELL TECHNOLOGY (MRVL)

Gap up and sell off to base

Minor Support

20ma

WRB breaks Support And 30 minute lows...

Many traders short this break down. This is the second biggest mistake traders make.

Avg. Vol: 3,086k

5 MINUTE CHART

Let's spend some more time on figure 7-7. Note it is in an uptrend. We have parallel rising 20 and 40 period moving averages (r20/40ma). Now it appears obvious it bounced off a nice support area. Looking back, it is easy to peg this as a long. A stock that gapped up, filled the gap, did a 15-minute Pristine Buy Set-up (see Appendix A) and continued higher.

Maybe now, you look back at the first chart and deny you ever would have shorted that pattern. Perhaps you would not have. Actually, traders try to short this set-up so much, it is the second most common mistake they make. Be aware that you can take advantage of other people's mistakes by playing this long at the right time. Watch for your reversal times—they can make your trading all the more successfull.

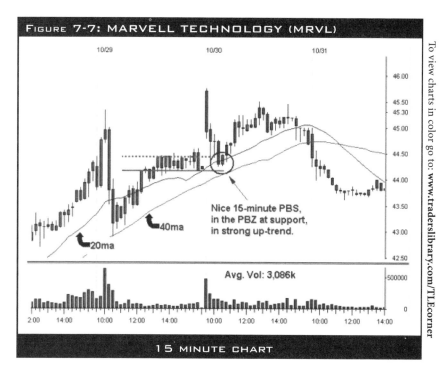

FIGURE 7-7: MARVELL TECHNOLOGY (MRVL)

Nice 15-minute PBS, in the PBZ at support, in strong up-trend.

40ma

20ma

Avg. Vol: 3,086k

15 MINUTE CHART

To view charts in color go to: www.traderslibrary.com/TLEcorner

A Strategy Against the Trend

By now, you know that I am a big fan of the saying, 'The trend is your friend'. We teach that 92% of your trades should be with the trend of the major stage. Buy quality pullbacks and consolidation breakouts in strong uptrends. Sell short rallies and consolidation breakdowns in downtrends.

However there are a few strategies that go against the trend. The climactic set-ups can be used to try to capture the quick bounce from an overdone situation. We also seem to go against the trend on transitions between stages, on the Minor Time Frame when the Major Time Frame has come into a buyable area. For example, you feel like you are buying a 15-minute downtrend when you buy a pullback on the daily chart. You are in fact playing the pullback on the daily chart that is in an uptrend.

Here is another play that goes against the trend. It is a favorite of mine, but they are hard to find. It is called an 'anticipatory breakdown of a high-of-the-day base, when the market is falling apart'. Sorry, no cute name for that one. The name states the whole strategy. Figure 7-8 is the 15-minute chart of NVDA and of the QQQ (the tracking stock for the NASDAQ 100) being used to represent the market since NVDA is a NASDAQ stock. They are aligned vertically, so you can compare relative strengths and weaknesses at a glance. You should consider doing this on your charts.

The concept is simple. On a bearish day, the weakest of all stocks will fall before the market does. They lead the market down. Then, the majority of the stocks move with the market. They are the market. Finally, if the market stays weak, more and more of the once strong stocks will begin to weaken and break down. How many times have you bought a base breakout at the wrong time, only to get stopped out? Well, this is taking the 'lemons' and making 'lemonade.'

Note that NVDA was a strong stock intraday. If you were on a 2-minute chart, you would see a stock basing at the high of the day while the market was falling. Note, however that on the 15-minute chart shown, NVDA is still in a downtrend at the time. The QQQ rally during lunch (arrow) could not make NVDA break above the base in any significant way. As the market completes a Pristine Sell Set-up (see Appendix A) into the Declining 20-Period Moving Average, NVDA pulls off a double top high. The market is in an all out downtrend, and NVDA could not show the strength it needed during the market rally.

So at the first sign of not breaking out, we short sell as early as possible. In this case, below the green bar that forms the double top (2x) high. Aggressive? Yes. Does it always work? No. Why is it attractive? Look at the stop. Often this is done with a five to ten cent stop, making the drop very worthwhile.

FIGURE 7-8: NVDA (TOP) & QQQ (BOTTOM)

Anticipating a Short of a "High of the Day Base"

20ma

40ma

2x Top High @ d40ma & mR

Short the 2x Top PSS or lower high

While NVDA was at the high of the day, it was still in a down trend and offered a tight stop as the QQQ below, was very weak...

20ma

40ma

QQQ at 15 Min PSS

While the QQQ confirmed a downtrend under prior day's lows, with a rising TRIN (not shown).

15 MINUTE CHART

To view charts in color go to: **www.traderslibrary.com/TLEcorner**

If you are going to go against the trend, you need an edge. They are lower odds trades by nature. The edge here consists of three things. First, the bigger time of NVDA was not bullish. Second, never fight the market unless your stock is unique for some reason; the market here was bearish all day. Third, the tight stop allows for some failures, yet still makes this a successful strategy.

Playing a Climactic Reversal

I would like to use this Lesson to review a trade strategy that can be a helpful tool in your trader's toolbox. It is also frequently misplayed and misunderstood. It is the "climactic buy" or "climactic sell" set-up.

This is one of the few strategies we have for playing a stock against the existing trend of the time frame you are playing. You should focus the majority of your plays on playing with the existing trend.

This play involves a stock getting extended a great distance in one direction and needing to correct. This can happen on any chart. We are going to take a look at an intraday Climactic Buy Set-up (CBS) on the 15-minute chart of Cephalon (Figure 7-9).

All of the following items made this an interesting play (note the corresponding numbers on the chart):

1. The stock had 5 lower highs on this time frame. This can include the prior day.

2. The distance from the declining 20 period moving average became extended.

3. The stock formed a reversal bar, a "changing of the guard' in this case.

4. An increase in volume came in at the low of the drop.

5. This happened at a reversal time, 10:00 AM EST.

The entry would be based on trading above a prior bar's high, once all the above are set-up properly. In this case, the entry would be over $45.94 with a stop under the low of the day at $45.00. For a target, we look for a "retracement" target. We look for about a 50% retracement of the fall, and find a resistance point to use in that general area. Often the declining 20 period moving average is in this area and can be used. That area in this case would be $46.50.

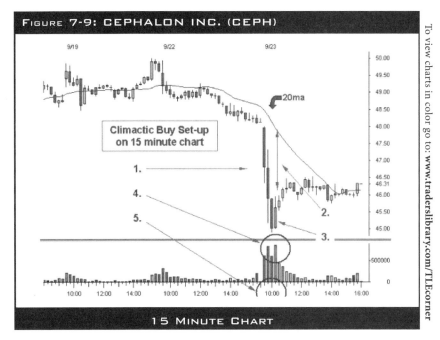

While this target was hit, the problem here is the risk reward. Sometimes, the reversal bar gets large and makes the stop wider and the target smaller. Often times, traders will 'zoom down' to a smaller time frame to find an entry. Note this is only acceptable when the bigger time frame (the 15-minute in this case) has properly set up. Look at the 2-minute chart below, for the same time period (Figure 7-10).

The idea here is to find the first moment the trend changes on the smaller time frame, once the bigger time frame is in the 'area' you expect the reversal to happen. You could use a 5-minute chart also. This technique is aggressive and will result in more stopped plays. However, the risk reward will be enhanced. In this case, the entry was over $45.55, stop either under $45.05 or $44.90. Let's take a quick look at how the entry was found.

Note the numbering on figure 7-10. Point 1 is simply a lower low in a downtrend as we expect. Point 2 is a lower high. Point 3 sets up a higher low for the first time, but this is not enough to act on. The trend does not change until we have two higher lows and two higher highs, and even being aggressive we want to see at least one of each before we act. Point 4 returns to a lower low, so no action. Point 5 makes a higher high (note, a challenge of the prior high is sufficient even if it does not break). Point 6 makes a higher low, and we now have a higher high and higher low. Aggressively, the PBS at point 6 can be the entry, or you can wait to trade over point 5 to make sure a second higher high is formed. This micro managing is only being done because based on the 15-minute chart, we are in the 'area' we expect a turn.

Remember to stay with the trend for almost all of your plays, but when you find a set-up similar to this one, use it as a guide to capture profits.

The Lunch Time Fade

In this lesson we are going to review a specific intraday strategy. It is called 'fading' a stock, meaning to play against the primary move. You would be

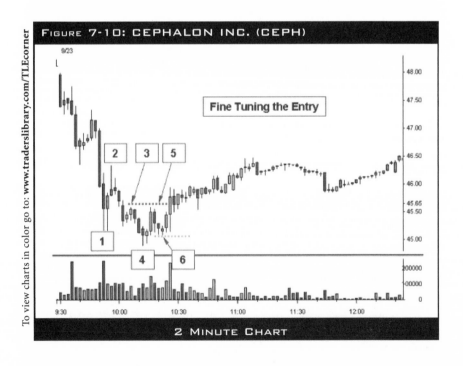

Figure 7-10: CEPHALON INC. (CEPH)

To view charts in color go to: www.traderslibrary.com/TLEcorner

shorting if there was a strong primary move to the upside. You would be going long if there was a strong primary move to the downside. You need to understand that you are trading against the short term trend.

We do not usually go against the short term trend, so make sure you understand this play. There are three requirements to keep in mind when doing this. First, it is a scalp type of play. You are going with the 'profit taking move', that is all. Second, it is to be done only when the primary move is extended. Third, this extended move must also happen at a reversal time. Reversal times have been explained previously in Chapter 2 of this book. Basically, they are certain times of the day when the market tends to reverse its prior direction.

Let's take a look at a real play of a stock called Macrovision (MVSN). On the following page are the 15-and 2-minute charts. The play is taken from the 15-minute (or 5-minute is some cases) chart (Figure 7-11), and we drop to the 2-minute only to refine the entry point (Figure 7-12).

MVSN ran 3.50, and over 4.00, including the gap. It is a 20.00 stock, so that is about a 20% move. This is huge. If you look at the daily, you will see this is as big as the bars get. The stock rallies at open, then pauses for an hour. This pause, after the morning run, is playable long over the 30-minute high. Notice that the run lasts an hour, and produces four large green bars. On the last green bar, the volume spikes. This is a sign of large turn-over—the last of the buyers getting in, and getting in very late. This 'exhausts' the supply of buyers. It also runs into the 200 period moving average, a very powerful stopping point for extended stocks. All of these factors make the stock 'extended'. Notice this all happens at 12:00 PM, the beginning of lunch and a reversal time in itself.

Once you have identified the play, we turn to a shorter time frame chart to refine the entry. Playing under the 15-minute bar would get you in very late as a scalp. So in this example, we turn to a 2-minute chart. In the area we are looking at, there are several 2-minute bars with higher highs, and then a red bar with a topping tail. The next bar has a higher low, and

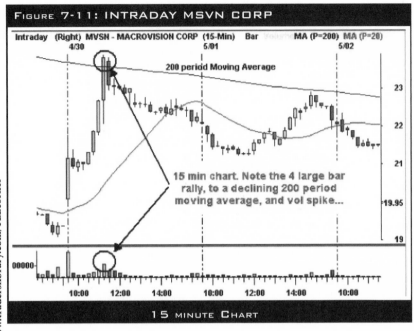

FIGURE 7-11: INTRADAY MSVN CORP

Intraday (Right) MVSN - MACROVISION CORP (15-Min)   Bar Volume   MA (P=200) MA (P=20)

200 period Moving Average

15 min chart. Note the 4 large bar
rally, to a declining 200 period
moving average, and vol spike...

15 MINUTE CHART

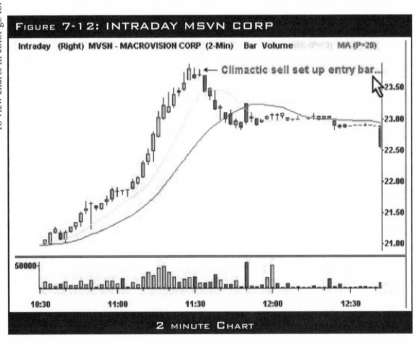

FIGURE 7-12: INTRADAY MSVN CORP

Intraday (Right) MVSN - MACROVISION CORP (2-Min)   Bar Volume   MA (P=20)

Climactic sell set up entry bar...

2 MINUTE CHART

a topping tail. The arrow is pointing at this last bar. Trading under this bar is the entry to the play, and the stop is the high of the entry bar or the high of the rally. This is known as a Climactic Sell Set-up (see previous section). For a target, you can do several things. The rising 20 period moving average on the 15-minute chart is often supported and is a good area to look at. You can also take all or half profits when a 15-minute bar trades above a prior 15-minute bar. You can also look to a prior base that may serve as support and a target.

So, the next time you're considering a stock to play, don't forget the lunchtime fade.

The Power of a Mortgage Play

On the second day of our Trading the Pristine Method® seminar, students learn a set of strategies called guerrilla tactics. One of the tactics that is taught in detail is known as a 'Mortgage Play'. It can be either 'Bullish' or 'Bearish', as is the case with all strategies. It involves a 'shock' that is delivered to a stock when it gaps a large distance to the other side of a '20/20 bar'. A bar that is exceptionally wide and has very little 'shadow' or 'tail' is known as a 20/20 bar.

If you look back at charts, you will find that quality high volume guerrilla tactics often change the nature of the daily chart for a long time to come. They often set a low or a high that lasts for a long time, and often produce a strong move from that area.

As with most things, there is a trade-off. With the good comes the bad. While a Mortgage Play can produce dramatic moves, the downside is the entry. The move can be very whippy and the safe stop that the play requires on the daily chart is the other side of the 20/20 bar. This can be a long way and therefore requires holding for a big target. Refer to a chart of CPRT from December 1, 2004 (Figure 7-13). To play the stock from the daily chart, the stop called for would be under the prior day's low. This is at the arrow marked 1. The entry is immediate.

Does this mean that only core traders (traders that hold positions for weeks or even months) need apply? Other risk-reward parameters can be used, but they have their pluses and minuses.

One option is to play the stock assuming it will move in one direction. It is not uncommon for the stock to open and quickly run hard in the desired direction. The problem can be that between pre-market and the opening minutes, it can move enough to make even an early entry seem late. Aggressive intraday traders may set the stop to the low of the current day at the time of entry. This is very aggressive and will lead to an above average number of stop outs, but can provide an incredible reward-to-risk ratio when successful. This is what was done in the PMTR for this play. The entry was the one-minute high, with the stop at the 1 minute low (low of day at the time of entry), which is at the arrow marked 2. The first target was easily taken on day one in this case, as the risk-reward justified the play.

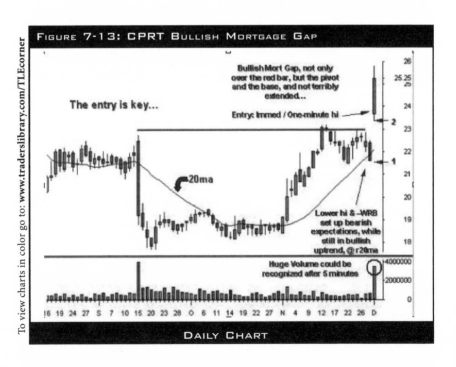

FIGURE 7-13: CPRT BULLISH MORTGAGE GAP

To view charts in color go to: www.traderslibrary.com/TLEcorner

Figure 7-14 shows the same stock two weeks later. A second target was taken on the rally the next day. The third target was taken on the secondary break-out on the daily chart, the last green bar shown. I would not be surprised to see this stock run much more, and a core position could also be held.

There is another way to play this strategy. It is to use the 'power' of the Mortgage Gap but to play the stock on an intraday basis, looking for a pullback and a set-up on a 5- or 15-minute chart. The advantage is a tight stop, similar to the last option, but played at a safer time, with less likelihood of a stop out. The disadvantage is that you may never get this pullback. You may just miss the play. Figure 7-15 is the 5-minute chart of CPRT for December 1, the day of the Mortgage Gap.

As you can see, at 10:00 Reversal time, CPRT pulled back and formed its first 5-minute Pristine Buy Set-up (see Appendix A). The intraday entry had a very tight stop afforded by the small green bar. This stop was not only tight, but also held as the stop for the remainder of the play.

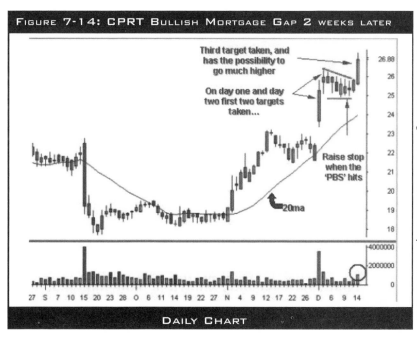

Figure 7-14: CPRT Bullish Mortgage Gap 2 weeks later

Play early with a quick entry and tight stop? Play early with a 5-minute entry and the wide stop from the prior day? Wait and play the first intra-day set-up? It is never an easy call. Some traders will look to play out two of the options. For example, try the most aggressive entry, and if it stops, replay on the first PBS intraday. The guerrilla tactics are powerful tactics and experienced traders can benefit on multiple time frames.

Finding Unique Plays

You may have seen explanations why the swing trading environment can be tough. I have written extensively about the need to recognize when daily charts become choppy, as a large battle will result in the area be-tween bulls and bears. The next logical question is: What does a trader do until the daily charts become more fluid? If you are with the markets all day, the obvious answer is to be very selective with any swing trades, and to focus more resources on intraday plays. Day trades, scalps,

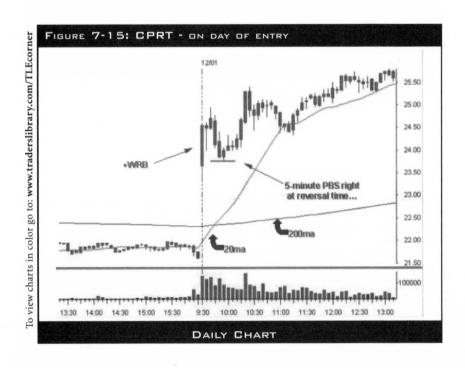

FIGURE 7-15: CPRT - ON DAY OF ENTRY

+WRB

5-minute PBS right
at reversal time...

200ma

20ma

DAILY CHART

guerrilla tactics, and using hourly charts for swing trading are all viable options.

If you cannot be with the market during the day, a couple of these options may still be available to you. Swing trading from hourly charts can be managed in a similar way to how you manage swing trading now. Also, there are many guerrilla plays that often are partially played out during the first hour of trading. If you can be with the market the first hour of the day, you may find the management of a guerrilla trade easy to handle. It is often the case that half the position is exited during the first hour, and a realistic raised stop can often be left on for the day. Calling in to check on the play late in the trading day may be all that is needed in some cases.

Another nice quality about guerrilla plays is that some of the plays are generated in part by gaps that occur in the morning. This is good because these gapped plays are often what we call, "on their own page." They do not necessarily follow the broader market. On many trendless or whipsaw days, this can be a blessing. The next chart is the daily chart of Sapient Corp. (Figure 7-16). We are focusing on the last day, the green bar. This chart was captured midday so it was not the closing chart.

The prior day was a bearish wide range bar (-WRB), in a downtrend, and everything about this stock looked lower. The next day, the stock gapped over the entire -WRB, which forms a guerrilla tactic known as a Bullish Mortgage Plan. It can be played with a wide stop, as this can often change the trend of the daily chart for many days or even weeks. It happens due to the shock value of the larger gap. Everyone who is short from the prior day, and in this case, the prior two weeks, is at a loss. That loss increases rapidly as the stock moves up, causing more to cover, and the circle begins. Also, at this point, the daily downtrend has been negated and we have longs from a variety of time frames jumping in the play. Due to all of these issues, a play like this will usually trade on its own merits, and ignore what the market is doing. People that short this stock are in pain; they don't really care what the market is doing.

Next question, is there any other way to enter besides a wide stop? If you were watching this stock for the first hour, a very nice intraday entry was offered that can often serve as both the entry and stop. Compare the two charts in Figure 7-17 (page 207), they are both 2-minute charts that show the opening on the last day on the daily chart (the gap up and green bar). On the left is the QQQQ, the NASDAQ 100 tracking stock, and SAPE on the right.

A tight base formed on SAPE into 10:00 reversal time. It pulled back once at 9:45 and based near the high. It refused to fill the gap and based at the high. Look at the relative strength. During this time the market (as viewed by the QQQQ) pulled back to fill a gap to a nice base in an uptrend. In other words, the market looked higher, but at its lows, SAPE was basing at the high. This makes the base entry with a tight stop (under the base or current low of day) a possible alternate entry.

As you can see, finding unique plays is not only possible, but can be profitable as well.

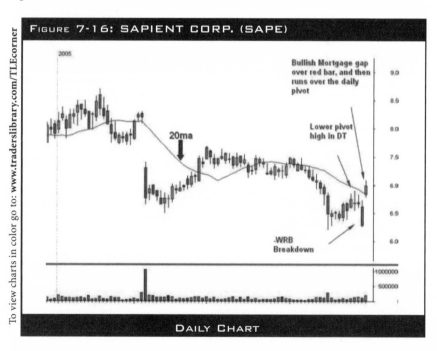

FIGURE 7-16: SAPIENT CORP. (SAPE)

DAILY CHART

Quality Breeds Nicknames

In recent articles, I have spent considerable time discussing the quality of the plays traders choose. This lesson will cover a few plays that have risen from taking a basic strategy, and adding some additional quality criteria. The result is a strategy that is more reliable and has earned the honor of getting its own nickname.

We are starting with a basing strategy. We will be looking on intraday charts, the 5- and 15-minute charts. The strategy I am showing you will also work on the 60, but rarely sets up on the daily. We will be looking for stocks that base, also known as consolidating, an area where the stock is resting, with a small range from high to low over several bars, preferably with very similar or even highs if looking to go long. The higher low is a plus. This gives it a sort of flat top. If looking long, we would also like the stock to be over the open price, over yesterday's closing price, and in the upper part of today's trading range. All the reverse is true if looking to short the stock. Figure 7-18 is an example of HLYW on a 15-minute chart. There is only a 10 cent range in that base.

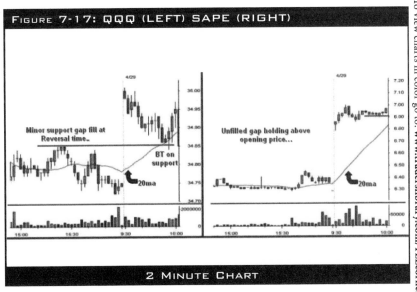

FIGURE 7-17: QQQ (LEFT) SAPE (RIGHT)

2 MINUTE CHART

After a stock has consolidated, there is a good chance that there will be follow through to the side of the breakout. It is also beneficial because your stop will be the other side of the base, making for a tight stop. You will be adding to the quality of the play if you have the above requirements as well. The stock is over yesterday's closing price and over today's open. It is also in the upper part of today's trading range.

Like all strategies, they don't always work. That is why we have stops. Adding some additional requirements can make this even a better play. Enter the 200 period moving average. This moving average is discussed in a previous lesson in Chapter 2, and is a very powerful moving average. Stocks will very often react to this moving average. Many rallies will end at the 200 MA; many falls will find support there. A base that forms right *under* the 200 MA can add some validity to the play that breaks over the base. When we add the 200 MA to the chart of HLYW, it looks like this (Figure 7-19).

Now this may seem a little counter intuitive. We teach that the 200 MA above a stock is resistance. It is. The question is how the stock handles that resistance. Stocks do not live exclusively on one side or the other

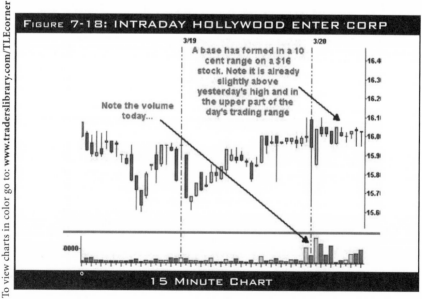

FIGURE 7-18: INTRADAY HOLLYWOOD ENTER CORP

3/19   3/20

A base has formed in a 10 cent range on a $16 stock. Note it is already slightly above yesterday's high and in the upper part of the day's trading range

Note the volume today...

16.4
16.3
16.2
16.1
16.0
15.9
15.8
15.7
15.6

.0000

15 MINUTE CHART

of the 200 MA. They do cross it. The thing to watch is how they cross. These are areas of opportunity. If a stock hits the 200 MA, pulls back, and then trades right back up to the 200 MA quickly, it is gaining strength. If every pullback finds support at a higher and higher level, that 200 has weakened to the point that it will give way. This resistance, when crossed, becomes a springboard now that all recognize that this stock wants to live on the other side of this moving average. This additional requirement has made this play known as the "Elephant Walk" in the Pristine Method® Trading Room.

Let's add another requirement and come up with another name. When will that price be likely to finally move over the base and 200 MA? Those who have studied what we teach know that any base is likely to move once enough time or price correction has happened to let the stock rest. This is measured in the afternoon by the 20 period moving average on the 15-minute chart. This is shown in red (Figure 7-20 page 211).

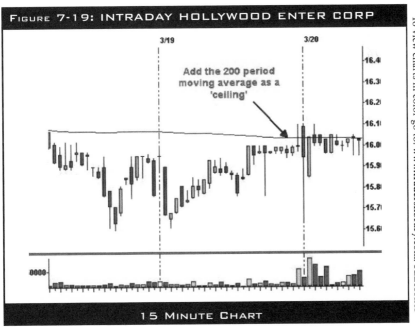

This kicks off the play by hitting the price and eventually crossing the 200 MA. Normally, the stronger moving average should win. The price is not agreeing as it is finding support on the 20 and not finding much resistance at the 200 anymore. This is the set up that shows the 200 MA is now going to give way and the price and 20 MA are going to cross and go above. With these two requirements now added, this play has earned the title of the 'Pinch Play' (Figure 7-21).

This is an example of starting with a good example and making it better. It applies to all charts, but you will find it most frequently on the 5- and 15-minute charts. It uses the 200 and 20 period moving averages only. If you only play the bases where you find this set up, your odds will improve greatly. The quality of the set-up matters greatly. Look for quality when looking at bases to play.

When it all Comes Together

In this lesson, we will examine a play where every detail could be the focus of a separate lesson. The focus of this particular lesson is what can happen when everything falls into place and multiple concepts converge. This brings buyers and sellers in extreme unbalance, and can have you anticipating the upcoming move.

The stock is Epicor Software Corp. Below is the daily chart, and our focus is the day of the gap up, July 20, 2005 (Figure 7-22 page 212).

On this morning, this stock came to my attention because it was on the gap list. A big focus of my morning is reviewing the stocks that are showing that they will be gapping up or down. These gaps can be the source of many strategies I teach. Depending on many factors, the stock may have a bullish or bearish bias once it begins trading. For EPIC, all of the following came together.

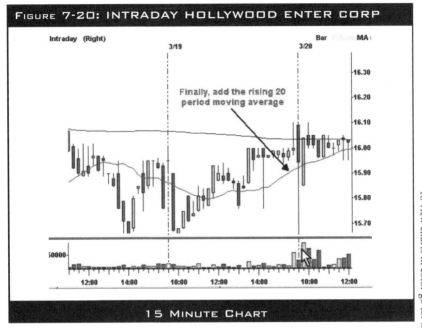

Figure 7-20: Intraday Hollywood Enter Corp

Finally, add the rising 20 period moving average

15 Minute Chart

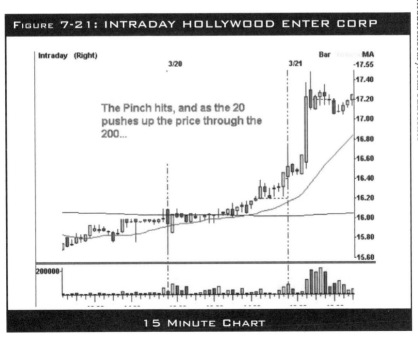

Figure 7-21: Intraday Hollywood Enter Corp

The Pinch hits, and as the 20 pushes up the price through the 200...

15 Minute Chart

The prior day, EPIC closed with a bearish red bar, (labeled 1), which had closed under the lows of the last six days. This pattern has traders leaning short into the close. The following day the stock opens (labeled 2) with a gap that not only clears the other side of the prior day's red bar, but also clears the prior pivots on the daily chart (the red lines). Now, just clearing the prior day's red bar created a minor bull mortgage play. This alone is enough to warrant a play.

The fact that we also cleared the pivots on the daily chart helped to confirm a professional type gap. Also, the gap was not so far that it was 'off the chart.' It just did enough to clear the resistance areas. While a gap of $1.20 on a $14.00 stock sounds excessive, gaps like this cannot be thought of as being extended. The reason is that no one has traded the stock in that void. When it opens pre-market, the stock trades at the gap price, and any pent-up demand for the stock must pay the gap price. No one has been able to buy it cheap, regardless of who wants it, they must pay the high price.

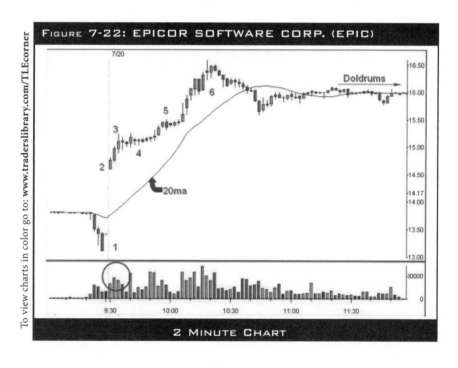

FIGURE 7-22: EPICOR SOFTWARE CORP. (EPIC)

2 MINUTE CHART

What could be better? The only thing better would be if the market was actually gapping down, and this day it was. This may sound backwards to some of you, to want the market gapping down when going long. There are two reasons we want this. First, this shows the stock has relative strength. The market is not causing the gap up. Second, much of this play is likely to play out in the first half hour. Even if the market heads lower, the chances of a market rally during the first half hour are good after a gap down, regardless of whether the market heads lower later or not.

All these things put together mean we want to enter this stock quickly, as there is a good chance that if it moves in the direction we want, it may do it right from the opening tick. There are many ways to play this. If playing off the daily chart, a wide stop is used. Sometimes day traders and scalpers will use the power of this move to justify a play with a smaller stop, or play both the day trade and the swing trade. Let's take a look at how I played EPIC that morning (Figure 7-23).

First, look at the 2-minute chart of EPIC (Figure 7-22) on the morning in question. You can see the end of the prior day ended with a sell off (labeled 1). The gap can be seen on the 2-minute chart, as EPIC opened at point 2. The entry could be immediate (make sure it is trading up) or you could use a one or two-minute high. Our entry was $14.82, with a 20 cent stop to the low of the day.

The rally and topping tail that formed at point 3 were used to exit a one-third lot as a scalp, at $15.15. The stock showed great strength as it coasted sideways into 10:00 reversal time. As the stock moved up, the stop was lowered to the base that formed at point 4, to lock in profits. Our second target was taken as the stock stalled at 5, $15.44. The ultimate day trading target was the $16.00 area, as that is where a weekly base formed a high (this is not shown here, refer to a weekly chart). Our last third was taken at 15.94 as the stock formed the red bar to the left of 6, the ultimate target.

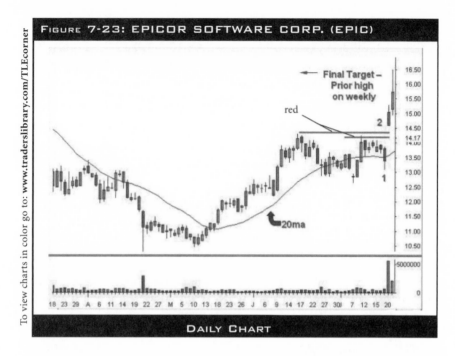

FIGURE 7-23: EPICOR SOFTWARE CORP. (EPIC)

DAILY CHART

While this was played out as a day trade, it could have also been used by swing traders as an entry, or a part of this position could have been saved as swing. When mortgage type gaps come with volume and clear resistance areas, this often changes the daily chart for months to come.

It was difficult to find fault with this trade, and when things come together like this, the play has good odds of working. They all don't work out like this one, of course, but trading is about playing the odds and, most importantly, learning your lessons.

Conclusion

In this book you'll find answers to the majority of trading decisions that will confront you as you trade on a daily basis. You have been shown what to expect, what to look for, and where to find valuable trading information. For the educated trader, well-laid plans are the key to trading success and this begins by studying the profession and paper-trading until you feel confident in your abilities to pick advantageous set-ups. Notice I didn't say pick winners, only recognize those situations that have high percentage chances of success coupled with low-percentage chances of loss. This is a controllable, not nerve-wracking—deductive, not presumptive—trading style.

Let's start with a review. Some things are common to all traders: You ought to be able to state your trading style and goals in a simple sentence. Why did you buy that stock? Your entry dictates your exit. Where is your stop? Will you make many small profitable trades—and sacrifice profits for smaller losses—or look for larger gains with larger risks? Remember, it has to make sense on paper if it's going to work for real. And finally, can you follow the trading plan that you've set up, and does it fit your personality?

Strategies for Profiting on Every Trade presents trading techniques unique to Pristine.com. As the market rises and falls, and reaches transition areas, there are ways to know whether the trend is likely bending or heading for the big plunge into no-man's land. Whether you use the system or incorporate key parts into your own trading, the concepts will give you additional interpretive skills, as well as improve your outlook and bottom line. The system's key points are shown below. Check for yourself and see if you're familiar with all of them.

1. Pattern recognition of a Level 2 trend.

2. Time frames. Which one are you using and do multiple time frames, particularly the larger ones, verify the direction of your trade?

3. Stops and money management. If it's high-risk, adjust the share size to keep losses at an acceptable level.

4. Timing the market—yes it is possible. The most important reversal times are at 9:50 – 10:10, 11:15, 1:30, 2:15 and 3:00.

5. Analysis of winning and losing trades. Did you sell your winning stock too soon? If it went wrong, why? Did you hang on too long to a losing trade or perhaps you never should have entered in the first place?

6. Market Direction. Ninety-eight percent of trades go with the overall trend of the market. The Semis lead the indexes. Recognize strengths and weaknesses in sectors and in stocks within the sectors.

7. Know your own abilities and frame of mind. Are you a beginner or "unconsciously conscious," quietly competent and in control?

8. Recognize several key tradable chart patterns and concepts: Opening gaps, trend lines, 20- and 200-period moving averages, support and resistance, wide ranging bars, tops and tails, 20/20 bars, and pullbacks.

9. Emergency management—What to do if your trade goes against you? How do you reset your stop-losses?

And finally don't forget the most common mistakes:

Don't short strong stocks.

Don't short multiple bar drops to support (or vice-versa).

Most importantly, as I stress throughout *Strategies for Profiting on Every Trade*, educate yourself, and set *yourself* up for success. While making decisions is largely intuitive, realize the competitive nature and uncertainty of the market. Examine yourself. Are you a high percentage player? Just like spotting that one chart pattern that will evolve into a winner, superior traders stand out in the universe of traders. May you come out a winner and on the right side of all your trades.

Appendix A

Analyzing Pristine Buy Set-ups

The Pristine Buy Set-up is one of the strategies we use to help determine buy set-ups. If you have taken the Trading the Pristine Method® seminar, you have undoubtedly learned all of the details and requirements of the Pristine Buy Set-up (PBS), as well as many other buy and sell set-ups.

The problem is, I have never talked to anyone who took the seminar who did not leave with their head spinning with information. By the time they put this information to use, some of the concepts are forgotten, or at least some details are fuzzy. This may lead to improper application of the strategy. One of the most common questions I take in the Pristine Method® Trading Room deals with improperly applying the PBS. The purpose of this article is to focus on the proper application of the Pristine Buy Set-ups (I will focus on "Buys" but this applies as well to the "Sell" equivalents). Also, all these tactics apply to all time frames, but I will be discussing PBSs on daily charts with swing trading in mind.

The Pristine Buy Set-up in its most powerful form has all of the following basic characteristics, the more, the better.

1. Stage 2 uptrend or at least a recent primary uptrend

2. Three-to-five day pullback

3. Narrow range day, or

4. A nice tail with a narrow body

5. Changing of the guard

6. Climactic volume

7. Previous major price support

8. Moving average support, and

9. Optional bonus—forming last two days of the month

There is not enough space in these lessons to review all of the requirements; however, many have been discussed in the previous lessons of this book. Even if you are not that familiar with all of the requirements, you have probably been trying to apply these techniques, and this article will help eliminate some mistakes you may be encountering.

The problem comes in when traders start looking for the picture of the PBS. They look for the 3-5 down bars to identify a potential PBS. The problem is that it is often all traders look for. In reality, this is only the beginning of the process. Let's look at the most common improper applications of the PBS.

First, the most common mistake is finding some or all of the requirements above, but ignoring the first one. If the stock is not in a Stage 2 uptrend, or at least a recent primary uptrend (recent high was a multi-month high), the strategy may not work as a swing strategy, meaning you cannot expect the stock to attack the prior highs. It may be played more as an intraday strategy, sometimes one day and overnight. After that, the pattern is not likely to have the strength to continue over the next couple days. This has been a common sight in recent months as there are not many stocks in true Stage 2 uptrends. Below is an example of a set-up that looks like a good PBS, but the stock is in a downtrend. You'll see the result (Figure A-1).

The second, is a cousin of the next chart (Figure A-2). It relies on only one or two of the above requirements. It happens when the stock is not in a primary uptrend, or when a series of lower lows and lower highs

FIGURE A-1: EARTHLINK INC

Daily (Right) ELNK - EARTHLINK INC   Bar Volume MA (P=20) MA (P=50)

Without the Stage 2 uptrend, even nice looking set ups can only be used for 1-2 days worth of gains...

Lots of things going for this PBS, tail to the 50 MA, narrow body, Pristine Buy zone, minor support...

DAILY CHART

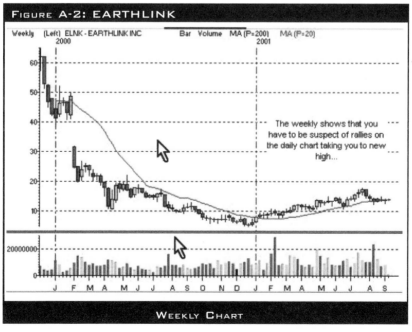

FIGURE A-2: EARTHLINK

Weekly (Left) ELNK - EARTHLINK INC   Bar Volume MA (P=200)   MA (P=20)

The weekly shows that you have to be suspect of rallies on the daily chart taking you to new high...

WEEKLY CHART

To view charts in color go to: **www.traderslibrary.com/TLEcorner**

has developed. It takes more to turn the short-term trend back to up, so relying on as many of the above requirements is important here. The mistake here is finding any 3-bar pullback and assuming that the pattern will hold. See RSTN below (Figure A-3). The pattern degrades from all time highs and never forms a set up that involves more than two or three of the criteria needed. The result is nothing more than 1-2 day bounces.

The third mistake is rarely talked about. The quality of the 3-5 bar pullback is very important. Ideally, the pullback should be 20-20 bars (little tails), no gaps, and all days have lower highs and lower lows. While technically, 3-5 lower highs is all that is required, you will find that the prettier the picture, the better the pattern. It is beyond the scope of this article, but just remember that gaps and tails may be trapping additional traders that may kill any upcoming rally. Check TTWO, (Figure A-4 page 223), which at the time was coming off all time highs, a strong sign. A clean set-up never develops and the stock cannot do better than a two day rally and a 50 percent retracement.

To view charts in color go to: www.traderslibrary.com/TLEcorner

Figure A-3: RIVERSTONE NETWORKS

Daily   (Right) RSTN - RIVERSTONE NETWORKS   Bar Volume MA (P=20) MA (P=50)

All time highs...

With nothing more, the down trend, even a short term one, is likely to continue...

Even coming off a stage 2 uptrend, a stock that has set a series of lower lows and lower highs, needs more than just 3-5 days down and a higher high. If played, these are only good for 1-2 days to the upside. There are countless examples of these on the charts.

18 21 26 25J 6 11 16 19 24 27 A 6 9 14 17 22 27 30 S 7

DAILY CHART

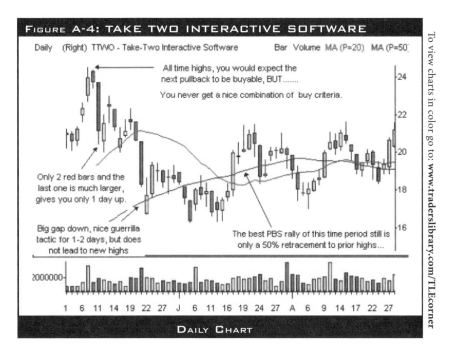

Figure A-4: Take Two Interactive Software

Daily (Right) TTWO - Take-Two Interactive Software   Bar Volume MA (P=20) MA (P=50)

All time highs, you would expect the next pullback to be buyable, BUT.......

You never get a nice combination of buy criteria.

Only 2 red bars and the last one is much larger, gives you only 1 day up.

Big gap down, nice guerrilla tactic for 1-2 days, but does not lead to new highs

The best PBS rally of this time period still is only a 50% retracement to prior highs...

To view charts in color go to: www.traderslibrary.com/TLEcorner

DAILY CHART

When you have a nice quality picture, you often get a better result. Check the uptrend in GILD on the weekly chart which follows (Figure A-5). Not many charts have this uptrend, which is the reason long swing trading has not been the place to be for a long time.

Now look at the same stock on the daily (Figure A-6). These moves were over the last two months. The power of being in a Stage 2 allows the stock the power to challenge prior highs.

Remember, the targets (attacking previous highs) on a Pristine Buy Set-up only apply when you have a quality set-up. If you are not in a quality Stage 2 uptrend, you do not have a quality set-up. A play may still be at hand, but the target will often be more along the lines of a guerrilla tactic or a one- to two- day rally. Remember also, many times a Pristine Buy Set-up is also a trigger for a quality guerrilla tactic, so there may be some overlap. This is why the target is often only a one- or two- day move unless the PBS is of the proper quality to move the stock to new highs. Hopefully, you now have a better understanding of all that is the PBS.

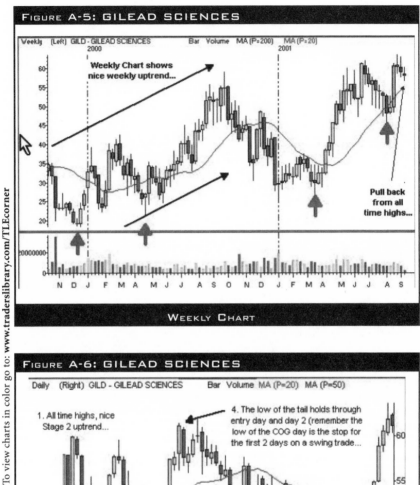

Figure A-5: GILEAD SCIENCES

Weekly (Left) GILD - GILEAD SCIENCES   Bar Volume MA (P=200)   MA (P=20)

Weekly Chart shows nice weekly uptrend...

Pull back from all time highs...

WEEKLY CHART

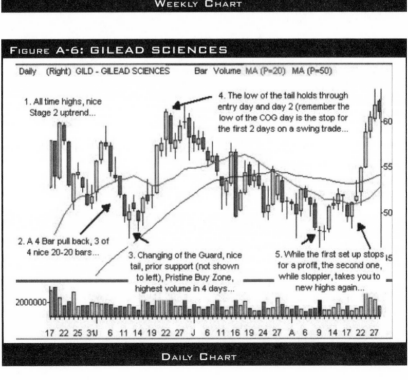

Figure A-6: GILEAD SCIENCES

Daily (Right) GILD - GILEAD SCIENCES   Bar Volume MA (P=20) MA (P=50)

1. All time highs, nice Stage 2 uptrend...

4. The low of the tail holds through entry day and day 2 (remember the low of the COG day is the stop for the first 2 days on a swing trade...

2. A 4 Bar pull back, 3 of 4 nice 20-20 bars...

3. Changing of the Guard, nice tail, prior support (not shown to left), Pristine Buy Zone, highest volume in 4 days...

5. While the first set up stops for a profit, the second one, while sloppier, takes you to new highs again...

DAILY CHART

Appendix B

Glossary

Basing   When the price of a stock has little or no trend.

Bear market   A period of time when the prices of stocks are falling or are expected to fall.

Breakout   When a stock moves through the stages of support and resistance, is followed by heavy trading and volatility in the market.

Bottoming tail   Points toward a low and is created by a stock dropping, then suddenly reversing to the upside.

Bull market   A period of time when the prices of stocks are rising, sometimes faster than they have in the past.

Climactic Buy Set-up   A type of trade that looks for stocks on daily charts that have recently experienced climactic declines on big volume, which renders them oversold and overdue for a strong rebound.

Core position   The longest time frame to hold a stock, sometimes lasting for months, where an exact exit strategy is planned.

Core traders   A trader who monitors weekly charts in order to hold positions for weeks or months, securing even larger profits.

Day traders   A trader educated in trading strategies and disciplines. Spends a good part of the day with the market and is trained to manage positions that may last from several minutes to several months.

Downtrend　The downward movement of a stock price or the market overall; the opposite of an uptrend.

ECN　An acronym for Electronic Communication Network. It is a system that brings buyers and sellers together for trading online.

ETF　An acronym for Exchange Traded Fund. Each ETF is a basket of securities that is designed to generally track an index (stock or bond, stock industry sector, or international stock), yet trades like a single stock. The most common are the QQQ, SPY, and DIA.

Fading　When fading a stock, you are playing against the primary move.

Futures　An obligation to receive or deliver a commodity or financial instrument sometime in the future, but at a price that is agreed on today.

Gap　Describes the condition when a stock opens at a significantly higher or lower price than its closing price on the day prior.

Guerilla trades　Tactics designed to capture fast moves in the market in one to two days.

HOLDRS　An acronym for Holding Company Depositary Receipts and are service marks of Merrill Lynch & Co., Inc. They are securities that represent an investor's ownership in the common stock or American Depositary Receipts of specified companies in a particular industry, sector, or group.

Income-Producing Account　Refers to an account that looks to take money out of the market everyday by executing day trades and guerrilla trades. These trades are designed to be exited the same day or one day and one night.

Index　A list of the larger, key stocks that are thought to be representative of the market itself. Some indices are the S&P 500, the NASDAQ 100, and the Dow Industrials .

Intraday   Describes price movements within the day or over the course of a single trading session.

Market maker   A trading firm that stands ready to buy or sell a particular stock on a regular and continuous basis at a publicly quoted price.

Market Volatility Index (VIX)   Provided by the Chicago Board of Options Exchange (CBOE) and is used as a guide to indicate the level of anxiety or complacency of the market.

Micro scalping   A trading strategy that attempts to make many profits on small price changes.

Mortgage play   A shock that is delivered to a stock when it gaps a large distance to the other side of a 20/20 bar, a bar that is exceptionally wide and has very little tail.

Moving average   Shows the average value of a stock's price over a set period. Generally used to measure momentum and define areas of possible support and resistance.

Pivot point   The average of a stock's high, low, and closing prices.

Pristine Buy Set-up   A strategy used to determine buy (and sell) set-ups, which has several specific characteristics to be successful (see Appendix A).

Protective stop   A strategy that aims to limit potential losses to a desired amount by using a stop-loss, or a point at which one will stop trading.

Pullback   A falling back of a price from its high.

Relative strength   Indicates when the stock is acting stronger than the market in general or stronger than the index it is in. An index can also have relative strength compared to the market.

Reward to Risk Ratio   The amount to be made from the entry to the target, as compared to the amount to be lost from the entry to the stop.

Resistance   A price level or area in which the demand for a stock will likely overwhelm the existing demand and halt the current advance.

Reversal times   Times during the trading day that the market is likely to stall or reverse the most recent pattern.

Swing trades   Taking trades with the intention of selling them after only two to five days.

Support   A price level or area in which the demand for a stock will likely overwhelm the existing supply and halt the current decline.

Topping tail   Points toward a high and is formed by a move to the upside, which then gives way to a sharp decline.

Trading plan   Defines what one wants to trade, when one wants to trade it, and how to trade and manage it.

TRIN   A measure of selling pressure; used as a market internal to measure the strength of the market.

Uptrend   The upward movement of a stock price or the market overall; the opposite of a downtrend.

Wide Range Bar (WRB)   A price bar that is much larger than the preceding price bars and therefore represents a trading period with higher volatility.

Zooming down   Going down one time frame to find an alternate entry to play.

Index

Trading Resource Guide

RECOMMENDED READING

SWING TRADING
by Oliver Velez

Oliver Velez, cofounder of Pristine.com and current CEO of Velez Capital Management, is renowned for his effective trading skills and specialized knowledge in technical analysis. His educational seminars are sought after by traders and often attended multiple times to extract every piece of wisdom from his presentations. Now, one of his most legendary sessions jumps from the screen into your hands in this coursebook of Velez's famed Swing Trading technique. With detailed text and a vivid 90 min DVD, you'll explore and master a highly profitable niche that exploits the two- to five-day holding period—a method too brief for large institutions, too lengthy for day traders, yet perfectly suited for individual investors with a mind towards success. In his captivating, high-energy style, Velez shows you how to:

- Spot opportunities using proven swing trading criteria
- Define periods of market uncertainty and make the right moves
- Discover key set-ups and effectively use moving averages
- Read charts successfully, especially Japanese Candle Sticks
- Win by going against conventional trading wisdom
- Understand and profit from understanding market psychology

Item #BCOVx5278311- $29.95

5 TRADING TACTICS THAT BEAT THE MARKET
by Oliver Velez

Finding profits in today's markets can be overwhelming. Now, one of the most sought after educators in the industry, Oliver Velez, cuts through the noise and hands you the five tactics that will get you to winning trades. From clearly seeing the trends in the chaos of market, to zeroing in on plays that are about to breakout and the key to significantly minimizing losses—this course hands you 5 of the most effective weapons to beat the markets.

Item #BCOVx5197571 - $99.00

TOOLS AND TACTICS FOR THE MASTER DAYTRADER: BATTLE-TESTED TECHNIQUES FOR DAY, SWING, AND POSITION TRADERS 1ST EDITION
by Oliver Velez and Greg Capra

A no-nonsense, straight-shooting guide from the founder of Pristine. com, designed for active, self-directed traders. Provides potent trading strategies, technical skills, intuitive insights on discipline, psychology and winning methods for capturing more winning trades, more often.

Item #BCOVx11221 - $55.00

MARKET WIZARDS
by Jack D. Schwager

What fellow traders are saying about Market Wizards:

"Market Wizards is one of the most fascinating books ever written about Wall Street. A few of the "Wizards" are my friends—and Jack Schwager has nailed their modus operandi on the head."

> - Martin W. Zweig, Ph.D., Editor
> The Zweig Forecast

"It's difficult enough to develop a method that works. It then takes experience to believe what your method is telling you. But the toughest task of all is turning analysis into money. If you don't believe it, try it. These guys have it all: a method, the conviction and the discipline to act decisively time after time, regardless of distractions and pressures. They are heroes of Wall Street, and Jack Schwager's book brings their characters vividly to life."

> - Robert R. Prechter, Jr., Editor of
> The Elliott Wave Theorist

> Item #BCOVx4050480 - $17.95

JAPANESE CANDLESTICK CHARTING TECHNIQUES, 2ND EDITION
by Steve Nison

This easy-to-read guide provides a clear understanding of Japanese Candlestick Charting, an increasingly popular and dynamic approach to market analysis. Steve Nison, known around the world as the "Father of Candlesticks, uses hundreds of examples that show how candlestick techniques can be used in all of today's markets. Traders will learn how candlestick charting can be used to improve returns and help decrease market risk.

Item #BCOVx 17304 - $100.00

MASTER THE STOCK MARKET

The market changes day to day...sometimes even minute to minute — so staying on top of your game is an absolute must. You need insightful, proven and time-tested investment tactics that can guide you to greater gains in every market condition. **And quite frankly, that's our specialty.**

We're Pristine.com, one of the world's most widely respected educational resources for independent traders. We're looking to build a nation of sophisticated, self-reliant investors who can handle, and who can profit from any market...anytime. **And we'd like you to be one of them.**

Pristine is no fly-by-night company. We have more than a decade of industry recognized expertise. Pristine's 12-year track record includes being ranked:

• Forbes' Best of the Web (2000)
• Barron's #1 Trading Web Site (1998)
• Stocks and Commodities Magazine Readers' #1 Choice for Training Center (2002)

But we don't want you to take our word for it. That's why we would like to give you a **FREE One Month Subscription** to our most popular newsletter services.

One FREE Month

The Pristine Core and Swing Trader Daily Newsletters

A $275 Value

NO RISK, NO OBLIGATION, NO KIDDING!

To register for your free month, call us today at:

800-340-6477

And be sure to mention this ad and offer code of TL-MONTH

FREE month offer is only available to first time customers of The Pristine Core and Swing Trader newsletter services.

There is a very high degree of risk involved in any type of trading. Past results are not indicative of future returns. Pristine Services, Inc. and all affiliated individuals assume no responsibilities for your trading and investment results. All comments made by Pristine instructors and representatives are for educational purposes only and should not be construed as investment advice regarding the purchase or sale of securities, options, futures, or any other financial instrument. Consult with a licensed broker or an investment advisor prior to making any particular investment or using any investment strategy.

NO LUCK NECESSARY!

Luck has nothing to do with making money on Wall Street. Increase your percentage of winning trades by knowing what to trade, when to trade, and how to trade. Whether you're a beginner, an experienced investor, or even a professional who trades for a living, the right training can help you achieve consistent profits from better investing. As an investor, you know the key to Wall Street success is reducing risk and maximizing profits. This is your chance to discover how to finally put those moneymaking odds in your favor. This is your opportunity to enhance your current investing techniques, master the art of stock trading, and ultimately make more money in the stock market.

Save $250 With This Ad

Register today and save $250 off the regular or early bird price of our two-day seminar, Trading The Pristine Method® Part I or II

100% Money Back Guarantee

If by lunch time on the first day of class, you are not satisfied for any reason with what we have provided, simply let your instructor know and you will receive a 100% refund of what you paid. No questions asked! By the way, lunch will still be on us.

**For More Information About Our $250 Discount,
Trading The Pristine Method® Part I or II,
and our 100% Money Back Guarantee,
Call A Pristine Counselor Today.**

877-999-0979

Or Visit www.pristine.com

Remember to use this offer code when placing your order either on the phone or online.

Offer Code: TL250

This book, along with other books, is available at discounts that make it realistic to provide it as a gift to your customers, clients, and staff. For more information on these long lasting, cost effective premiums, please call us at (800) 272-2855 or you may email us at sales@traderslibrary.com.